PASTORAL POETICS: THE USES OF CONVENTIONS

IN RENAISSANCE PASTORAL ROMANCES—

ARCADIA, LA DIANA, LA GALATEA, L'ASTRÉE

PASTORAL POETICS: THE USES OF CONVENTIONS IN RENAISSANCE PASTORAL ROMANCES—

ARCADIA, LA DIANA, LA GALATEA, L'ASTRÉE

Pilar Fernandez-Cañadas de Greenwood

Publisher and distributor
  José Porrúa Turanzas, S.A.
  Cea Bermúdez, 10 - Madrid-3
  España

Distributor for U.S.A.
  Studia Humanitatis
  1383 Kersey Lane
  Potomac, Maryland 20854

Printed in the United States of America
Impreso en Estados Unidos

Cea Bermúdez, 10 - Madrid-3
Ediciones José Porrúa Turanzas, S.A.

FOR DAVYDD AND ALEX

No se ven tantos rostros figurados
en roto espejo, o hecho por tal arte,
que si uno en él se mira, retratados
se ve una multitud en cada parte . . .

Erastro in Miguel de Cervantes,
La Galatea

ACKNOWLEDGMENTS

I would like to express my gratitude to those who assisted me in the preparation of this study. James Boon, William J. Kennedy, and Mary Randel read and commented on the work at various stages in its preparation. I particularly want to thank Alain Seznec for his critical reading and his kindness in encouraging me in the efforts that led to the publication of the study.

The manuscript was expertly prepared for publication by Mrs. Coraleen Rooney.

Lastly, my thanks to Bruno Damiani, editor of the series STUDIA HUMANITATIS.

TABLE OF CONTENTS

CHAPTER I

INTRODUCTION

Aims and Arguments of this Study

Within the general spectrum of our literary history, pastoral genres (1) occupy a somewhat mysterious and puzzling place. Greatly popular at various times in the history of Western literature, they flourished with particular impact during the latter part of the Renaissance, especially in the form of prose romances. Subsequently, e.g. in the eighteenth century and in the Romantic period, this literature resurfaced, although mainly in the form of adaptations of some major pastoral themes.

Despite an impressive body of studies ranging from general theories to particular analyses of individual authors and individual works, pastoral remains strangely difficult to grasp. The majority of the studies dedicated to pastoral indeed clarify pastoral themes, their origins, range, and implications, but when dealing with the poetics of this literature, most

---

(1) There are lyrical, dramatic, as well as narrative pastoral works. Strictly speaking, then, pastoral literature may cross genre boundaries, even combining several genres within a single work. In recent times, the application of the term genre to different modes and subgenres has gained acceptance. See also Chapter II, footnote 1.

critics conveniently dismiss the problematics of the issue by referring to the works of pastoral as conventional.

The use of particular sets of conventions is a characteristic of pastoral, but this global label of conventionality neither explains the actual processes of use and re-appropriation of conventions by the authors nor does this categorization suffice to distinguish among the actual conventions employed. Distinctions must be made and a careful analysis must be applied if we are to understand the defining characteristics and the aims of this remote genre.

The examination of some basic literary conventions and their interrelations as constitutive of Renaissance pastoral romances is the aim of the present study and the number of specific arguments to be made regarding this subject is quite large. To introduce this study, I will here only allude to those that receive extended development in the chapters that follow.

To begin with, it is necessary to deal with the concept of convention itself. Since the term convention is used to cover a wide range of issues, a preliminary distinction is called for. I am referring here to certain aspects of literary conventions, specifically to the explicit and implicit agreements by which works of literature are produced and the characteristics by which a given genre is recognized. A brief analysis of the concept of literary convention will also be contrasted with similar and related concepts: the *topoi*, the "dominant," and some connections with the theories of imitation and influence.

As any other literary genre, pastoral literature sought and maintained very specific conventions of its own. Established at its inception in Classical times, the conventions of pastoral are recognizable in the subsequent manifestations of the genre.

I do not defend or criticize the conventions of the genre. My argument is that we must understand the dynamics involved in the processes of reappropriation and readaptation of these conventions. The reasons for this are twofold. In

order to grasp the importance and understand the prolif-
eration of this, now remote, literature, it will be necessary
to place the works of pastoral in wider contexts as well as
to examine specific works in detail. In this study, this is
called the investigation of the interdependence of macro and
micro-contexts. Examples will be drawn from: Sanazzaro's
Arcadia (1504), Montemayor's *Diana* (1559), Cervantes'
La Galatea (1585), and d'Urfé's *L'Astrée* (1630-1638).

Among the most readily recognizable conventions of pastoral, two sets will receive special attention here. One is
comprised of the principles of coherence: correspondence
and balance among the elements of the compositions and the
ideas expressed in them. Those principles together with the
pursuit of beauty and euphony are part of the general conventions guiding the production of pastoral romances.
Throughout this study these principles of coherence, *vraisemblance*, will be stressed, particularly in connection with the
cultivated self-reflection on the role of pastoral poetry itself
and the recognition of the role of the poet in exercising and
reactivating the power of art.

The second set of conventions centers on the appropriation of linguistic, thematic, and structural features adapted
and repeated from earlier works of the pastoral genres. An
analysis of these conventions forms the core of Chapters III,
IV, and V.

Through a combination of the renewal of the works of
earlier authors by repeating and reappropriating their rhetorical and "pastoral" themes, and by the praise of the poets and
fellow participants in the art, authors, audiences, and works
are thus made part of a literary cycle. Recognizing themselves
as part of a series, both audiences and authors are made
aware that they belong to a cultural tradition in which they
actively collaborate. The very repetition and ornate complexity characteristic of pastoral poetics become arguments for
the greater appreciation of the power of art and of the artist.
Because I believe that this dynamic dimension at the center

of pastoral poetics has been generally ignored to the detriment of our understanding of this literature, it will receive a great deal of emphasis in this study.

I have chosen for detailed study *La Galatea*, the first fictional work of Cervantes, as representative of these arguments. Published in 1585, at the peak of the popularity of the genre, *La Galatea* well represents the special kind of activity involved in the production and understanding of literary art. For a pastoral work, this activity is a combination of experience, reflections on the aims of art, and skill. These are the basic requirements for understanding this literature. This enterprise is one of the aims announced and developed throughout the six *libros* of Cervantes' work.

The Plan of the Study

The study is structured along the analytical lines laid out in the present chapter. The second chapter develops the concept of literary convention as it applies to the pastoral works of the Renaissance. A distinction between this concept and those of *topoi*, the "dominant," and theories of imitation and influence completes the chapter.

The third chapter deals with the major linguistic conventions of pastoral. Repetition of character's names, of rhetorical expressions, and even of complete verses from earlier works is a major convention of pastoral romances. This form of intertextual association receives a great deal of attention in this study, not only for the peculiarities that it imparts to the works, but because it also shows the effort and knowledge required of the audiences of pastoral. Both the audiences and the authors are made participants in the interpretation and readings of the works in an especially active way. My argument is that, as a consequence of this convention of intertextual recuperation, the audiences of pastoral are incorporated in a field of associations that requires specific familiarity with works and authors of the genre as a whole. The third chapter also includes a brief analysis of the idylls and the eclogues, a discussion of some forms of recuperation and renewal of literary elements from previous pastorals, the use of category nouns, quotations and literary "découpages," and the description of some prominent forms of versification favored in the pastorals of the Renaissance.

In Chapter IV the major rhetorical conventions of pastoral are taken up. These include intensification, hyperbole, ellipses, synecdoques, hyperbaton, and simplification. The analysis of these conventions is not intended as an all-inclusive catalogue of the rhetorical conventions found in pastoral romances. These groups of conventions are selected for examination in relation to the role they have as vehicles of expression, functioning within the *vraisemblance* of the works and the genre.

In Chapter V an analysis of the basic conventional themes developed in pastoral is integrated with the previous analysis of the linguistic and rhetorical conventions. A detailed examination of the themes of fortune, time, love, and nature is followed by the study of the conventional pastoral melancholy.

Finally Chapter VI concludes the study with a detailed analysis of the integration of pastoral conventions in Cervantes' *La Galatea* in which the questions of innovation and typicality come to a clearer view. In this reading of *La Galatea* all the analytical work from the earlier chapters is put into play. This analysis and recapitulation of the argument will provide a coherent view of the uses and re-elaborations of the different conventions of pastoral. By integrating the conventions of language, rhetorical forms, and thematic concerns within the particular "nested" structure of *La Galatea*, I endeavor to arrive at a fuller assessment of the artistic and cultural values of this seminal Cervantine work.

CHAPTER II

THE CONCEPT OF CONVENTION

The Misuse of Convention

Pastoral literary genres (1), most particularly the pastoral narratives that flourished during the Renaissance, have been consistently described as "highly conventional." Indeed it has become "conventional" among the many scholars of pastoral literature to define the genre by alluding to the strong reliance of pastoral authors on conventions. Statements such as the following abound: ". . . the heroic verse [became] an appropriate vehicle for the *highly conventionalized* and stylized

---

(1) For convenience and brevity, I shall follow the definition of the pastoral genre proposed by Mia Gerhardt in her comprehensive study: "Le mot 'genre', dans cette combinaison des oeuvres prend une acception à la fois plus libre et plus restreinte que son acception ordinaire de 'genus' au sens d'Aristote. Là, c'est la forme qui décide: genre épique, genre dramatique. Dans des expressions comme 'genre pastoral' genre picaresque' cependant, le mot genre indique l'ensemble de toutes les oeuvres, quelle que soit leur forme, qui *traitent d'une certaine manière de bergers*, de 'picaros' . . . *Essai d'analyse littéraire de la pastorale dans les littératures italienne, espagnole et française*, Assen, Van Gorcum & Comp., 1950, p. 21, emphasis mine. I have stressed the certain peculiar way of treating the conventional shepherds because it is precisely this that I want to elucidate in my study.

pastoral." (2); "The story recited by Sincero in chapter 7, however, strikes one as *extremely conventionalized*, and it is difficult to believe that a love for Carmosina Bonifacio was any compelling motive in the composition of Arcadia." (3); ". . . the bucolic eclogue . . . a form based upon artificiality and convention . . . (4). The term "convention," then, as used in these statements, forms part of the definition of the pastoral genre. But the identification of pastoral with conventionality *per se* creates an insufficiently analytical conception of pastoral literature by stressing the role that conventions play in the elaborate pastoral aesthetics without explaining how they actually operate in relation to each other.

To assert that pastoral literature is conventional is an empty statement since literature by definition is based on conventions. Literature, as Valéry has said, is among all the arts ". . . the one in which conventions play the greatest role." As Culler (1975:116) (5) notes, the cultivation of a particular type of literature is only possible because of the existence of literature itself. Literature is inconceivable without a wide set of cultural understandings. Thus what matters is not the existence of conventions, but how particular conventions represent innovation, adaptation or even subversions of earlier contexts that achieve one of literature's main goals: the creation of fictional characters experiencing an equally fictional world.

Although specific literary conventions play an important role in the elaboration of pastoral works, labeling pastoral

---

(2) W. Leonard Grant, *Neo-Latin Literature and the Pastoral*, Chapel Hill, University of North Carolina Press, 1965, jacket copy.

(3) Jacopo Sannazaro, *Arcadia & Piscatorial Eclogues*, translation by Ralph Nash, Detroit, Wayne State University Press, 1966, translator's introduction, p. 8.

(4) Walter W. Greg, *Pastoral Poetry and Pastoral Drama*, London, A. H. Bullen, 1906, p. 13.

(5) Jonathan Culler, *Structural Poetics*, Ithaca, Cornell University Press, 1975.

literature, or any other as "extremely conventional" has the negative effect of dismissing the works in question (or some relevant elements in them) as mere parts of some arcane and vague context. This act removes the responsibility for any direct and serious study of them as part of a total cultural pattern. The result, regardless of the theoretical school being followed, is an atomized analysis of one or several elements identified as persistent or recurrent, reducing pastoral to unidimensionality. No matter how thoroughly and cleverly the analysis is done, it fails to offer a unified picture of the general aesthetics that necessarily lie beneath or behind the surface.

Defining pastoral works as "highly conventional" also implies that the genre is static, closed, without vitality. We can see this in statements like the following about the pastoral of the Spanish Golden Age: "Cervantes is admittedly a wonderful creator, but the pastoral of his time—a pastiche or mosaic of conventional figures—gave him no opportunity to display his powers as an inventor" (6). This kind of assessment represents a closed attitude that can and often does lead to a genuine avoidance of the direct study of the works in question.

When reading pastoral works such as *Arcadia, La Galatea, L'Astrée*, modern readers are confronted with acknowledged masterpieces of a past age which present challenging problems of interpretation. Although they coexist with other types of literary expression (epic, picaresque, meditative poetry, chivalric novels, among others), they represent a particular way of stressing artistic artificiality which sets

---

(6) *The Complete Works of Miguel de Cervantes Saavedra, Vol. II: Galatea*, Jas Fitzmaurice-Kelly, editor, H. Oelsner and A. Welford, translators, Glasgow, Gowans and Gray, 1903, quoted from the editor's introduction, p. xxxiv. For more statements of this sort, consult Fleming G. Vinson, *A Critical Bibliography of the Spanish Pastoral Novel* (1559-1663), unpublished Ph.D. dissertation, University of North Carolina at Chapel Hill, 1969.

them apart from other literary genres and modes. Pastoral romances are based on a complex intertextual recuperation of already known characters, plots, themes, and even specific language. These intertextual references make very evident the fact that these works are part of a literary and cultural cycle. In this way, pastoral addresses the eternal questions about the character and purpose of the whole artistic enterprise itself.

Thus despite their distance and strangeness for us, we cannot dismiss pastoral works with a glib reference to conventionality. They demand interpretation and the restoration of their possible meanings. For modern audiences this is a challenge because we must make coherent interpretations of unfamiliar objects and sets of still-present and forgotten conventions and it is a duty because we must add to the chain of readings, renewing these messages which are such a puzzling legacy. And we must do this without foreclosing interpretations of these works with the vague label of conventionality for this defeats the very effort to understand them.

Another consequence of categorizing pastoral works as "conventional" is to identify these literary productions with that which is artificial, false, and thus opposed to the realistic, more true to life kinds of literature. Yet this misses the very point of pastoral.

To violate the principles of naturalistic art and to place action on another level of reality—the fantastic, extraordinary qualities of fictional reality—is the core of pastoral art and it will be discussed below. This is important for my study because these violations were themselves an innovation, one that was particularly elaborated by the authors of pastoral in the late sixteenth century and the first half of the seventeenth century, authors who stressed and prove the importance of imagination in the literary arts. In this, they succeeded in creating another confluence of neoplatonic concepts (inspiration, beauty, cult of the many facets of feeling) with the still enduring Aristotelianism (mimetic forms, literary standards of appropriateness, *decorum*) (7).

After all, it is precisely in the opposition between fiction and reality that the crucial role of the artist and the meaning of artistic creations come into clear view. That artists were aware of the dialectic existing between literary texts and the empirical world is well known. This dialectic was at the center of Aristotelian aesthetics and was of continuing concern for Renaissance theorists such as Giraldi (*Dei romanzi*), Nebrija (*Gramática castellana*), Tasso (*Dell'art poetica*), Sidney (*Defence of Poesy*) and many others. Cervantes, himself author and critic of pastoral tales and pastoral themes, often underlined the opposition between appearance and reality, truth and fictionality (e.g. *Don Quijote, El coloquio de los perros*, and others (8). This particular balance of opposites is at the root of Cervantine aesthetics.

In sum, pastoral (unrealistic, fictional) aesthetics stress the dichotomy between a naturalistic concept of art and the imaginal force of that which is fictional. The resulting gap between these naturalistic and imaginal realities is made obvious in the reliance of pastoral works on conventions of form, theme, and above all, on the strange enclosure that their

---

(7) *Decorum*, Latin, neut. of decorus; that which is seemly, orderly. Esp. in dramatic, literary, or artistic composition; that which is proper to personage, time, or subject in question, or to the nature, unity or harmony of the composition; fitness, congruity. *The Oxford English Dictionary*, Oxford, Oxford University Press, 1969. A discussion of the ideas of harmony in the composition as interpreted by sixteenth century writers such as Alonso López Pinciano in his *Philosophia Antigua Poética* (1596) is provided below. For Cervantes' interpretation of the principles of artistic *decorum* see Chapter VI below.

(8) Miguel de Cervantes, *Don Quijote de la Mancha*, I, XXV, especially p. 238, and II, LXXII, especially pages 1060-1062. Martin de Riquer, editor, Barcelona, Juventud, 1958, and *Novelas ejemplares de Miguel de Cervantes*. Leonardo G. Morelos, editor, Garden City, New York, Doubleday and Co. Inc., 1962.

stilted, clicheified language creates against almost any simplified and reductive interpretation.

Similar artistic operations have been recently studied in symbolist literature, Flaubertian aesthetics (Culler, 1974) and the uses and functions of the cliché (Holdheim, 1978; Riffaterre, 1960, 1963). Though not exclusive to pastoral, in pastoral they constitute a nearly perfect example of the refined, self-contained approach to art. The pastoral approach, in its own way, illuminates the power of art as much as do the excesses and distortions of baroque aesthetics or the minute detailed realistic approaches of picaresque. They each emphasize different aspects of the artistic enterprise.

The rules and principles of pastoral correspond to a specialized conception of art that is remote from contemporary readers. Therefore the unraveling of these rules and principles presents a definite analytical challenge.

To obtain a deeper understanding of the rules at work in pastoral aesthetics, I propose to focus precisely on the different kinds of pastoral conventions, on the ways these operate in some representative pastoral narrative works, and finally, on the way these conventions are adapted and renewed in these representative works. Rather than dismissing this strange and remote aesthetics with a glossing reference to "conventionality," I will take a close look at the distinctive conventions and processes by which these conventions are operated and incorporated at different levels in the total structure and message of the works.

Convention Defined

The label conventional is used by literary critics as a cover term for a variety of phenomena, however the term is also applied in ordinary discourse in a wide variety of ways. Its use extends from everyday, common language (9) to the language

---

(9) Current usages of the word include positive as well as negative connotations. It is used as an equivalent of normal, familiar, old-fashioned, unimaginative, wooden, conformist, etc.

of journalism, advertising, politics and the arts. Most of these usages conform to the meaning of the Latin verb *convenio-vēni-ventum* in its intransitive form: to agree, to gather (10). In this way the word applies to the terminology of current American politics—to gather at a predetermined location to select a representative individual or party by means of common agreement, i.e. vote (11). For all areas of its use, including literary criticism (12) the meaning of the Latin verb *convenio* in its transitive form is pertinent as well: to incorporate something or somebody to the mainstream (*in manum o viro in manum convenio*, to incorporate the wife to her husband's —institution of marriage—jurisdiction); to find something or someone along the way (*convenio aliquem in itinere*) (13).

Thus, convention holds a double meaning: creating an agreement that contains within itself the feelings, ideas, or aspirations of a particular group, country or historical period, and the act of incorporation by general agreement, in this case, into the linguistic and cultural mainstream. These agreements do not necessarily have to be expressed or legislated, but they are collective and strongly binding nonetheless.

Since the term embraces a wide spectrum of fields and areas, I will delimit its application here. To support my analysis of pastoral conventions in the pastoral narratives of the

---

(10) *Diccionario ilustrado latino-español*, Barcelona, Spes, 1950, my translation.

(11) Although legal language shares in the meaning of this term, referring to a precedent or pretried case by which a consensus or agreement within the law is reached, the intention is entirely normative and I take the term in a less restrictive sense.

(12) The best classification of the conventions as applied to the literary theory of poetic reading is in the comprehensive study by Jonathan Culler, *Structuralist Poetics, ed. cited*. His five levels of *vraisemblance* or ways that enable works to be interpreted according to a structural method are most useful, precisely in the implied relationship of a given work to a macro-textual and inter-textual set of pre-established agreements. See especially Chapter 7. See also W. Leonard Grant, *op. cit.*, pp. 37, 70.

(13) *Diccionario ilustrado latino-español, op. cit.*, my translation.

Renaissance, I will use convention in two major senses: as general contexts and as specific elements. The general contexts refer to concepts about the nature and role of art as an instrument of knowledge. The specific elements may consist of linguistic expressions, such as the Spanish *discreción* or the Italian *sprezzatura,* and "pastoral names (Tityrus, Galatea). They can also refer to particular forms (idylls, eclogues) or themes (e.g. unrequited love).

Once established, these impart their characteristics to the genre itself. In pastoral literary works, the formal, linguistic, and thematic conventions often come to represent the essential characteristics of the genre as a whole—e.g. the theme of the Golden Age is equated with pastoral, as is the presence of nymphs, metamorphic episodes, the "nested" episodic structure of the narratives, and the dramatic character of the eclogues.

Durability of Conventions

A difficult question crucial to the selection and acceptance of conventions centers on the reasons, purposes, and specific factors contributing to their establishment or abandonment. The goal of explaining this process is avidly pursued but seems always to lie beyond reach. Yet we know that some conventions disappear from the literary mainstream while others enjoy a more prolonged life.

There are many causes at work here. Part of their durability arises from their being very clearly identified with a particular form (as in the case of the Petrarchan sequential use of the sonnet), with an author (Virgil's Eclogues), or with a genre (the eclogue and the idyll, for instance). But conventions are much more than just a trait or characteristic preserved in time. They also embody the form and meanings associated with the genre proper and as such they endure.

A clear case is found in some of the thematic conventions of pastoral which, although typically found in the Renaissance, have been adopted at other times and have expanded their generic characteristics to works dealing with related themes. Examples of this durable type of convention are the theme of the *locus amoenus* and some of the elaborate rhetorical figures—hyperbaton, paranomasia, paradox—used in sixteenth and seventeenth century pastorals as well as in the works of poetry and drama of other genres in the Baroque and in other literary periods.

There are even broader instances where certain characteristics are extended to all the literary institutions of the day and even to other arts. This happened during the Baroque to the "cultism," "serpentine representations," "conceptisms," and the like, that, affected not only the literatures of Europe, but the visual, performing, and functional arts as well. The same could be said of the conventions of the Elizabethan period in England and the Neoclassic and Romantic periods in all of Europe as well.

Conventions do not operate in a vacuum; this fact underlies their integrative quality. Involved in larger systems or contexts, they serve as vehicles and embodiments of elements constituting a "consensus" that gives rise to the recognizable pattern we call styles, periods, "spirit of the age," and any of the multiple "isms" and schools. This phenomenon, affecting various ideologies, has been studied by philosophers (e.g. Dilthey's *Geisteswissenschaften*), literary historians, historians science (e.g. Thomas Kuhn), and social theorists (e.g. Antonio Gramsci).

As a note of caution it is very important to stress that even when we understand conventions as a total body of theories and aesthetic directions, we must remember that the same basic consensus did not produce just one or even a few similar major styles and generic trends. Many styles and genres coexist within the bounds of the same general consensus.

Orientation and General Framework of This Study

The use of certain theoretical orientations and frameworks is necessary to organize the body of analysis to be presented in this study. Inevitably such theoretical structures are more coherent than the reality they seek to comprehend. Throughout an attempt will be made to keep the theoretical formulations resolutely in their role as tools of research, useful but dangerous if believed in too fervently. Certainly mechanistic applications of theories have already ruined many research efforts. In what follows I will simply set out the universe of terms I will employ and will review my central assertions about pastoral.

A central distinction within my theoretical framework is comprehended in the terms "macro-contexts" and "micro-contexts." The general macro-contexts or conventional general themes—such as the acceptance of art and the cultivation of beauty, the cult of love, and introspection and self-knowledge—are important. Used to answer the human desire for knowledge, they were new, important, and widely accepted epistemological tools. Knowledge of these macro-contexts is crucial to an understanding of pastoral; they will be dealt with in detail in this study.

Yet a study of them alone does not suffice to explain the existence or the immense popularity enjoyed by pastoral narratives during the sixteenth and seventeenth centuries in Europe. Necessarily complementing an examination of macro-contexts is a study of micro-contexts or conventionalized linguistic and stylistic forms. These too are crucial for the understanding of pastoral and for placing it in the context of other concurrently popular genres.

Three main elements are associated with the pastoral genre proper. First, there is the cultivation of an extremely stylized and beautiful language as mark and sign of true artistry. Within this there is yet another micro-textual level where the units are the most specific, technical elements—such as the recurrent metaphors, verbal expressions, versification meters, arrangements of rhetorical figures (paranomasia, *adynaton* hyperbaton) and the use of ballad, romance, and other forms employed in the various vernacular languages and dialects. Secondly, there is the consistent and carefully-patterned use of particular themes, figures, and allusions belonging to a more or less well-defined classical and mythical past—such as the appearance of nymphs, the myth of the Golden Age, etc., —and the following of forms and styles of masters of the past. Finally, there is the minute observation and discussion of the problems of Fate, Love, and Death set against a crystallized, stilted background of Nature.

These basic elements or micro-contexts are often considered by literary critics and students of pastoral literature also as *the* conventions of the pastoral genre, making it extremely difficult to distinguish among the various sub-categories of conventions themselves (14).

Each of these contexts and elements is important, even crucial, for understanding pastoral and relating it to other concurrently popular genres. The study of none by itself is sufficient. An adequate approach must blend attention to the macro- and micro-contexts.

The complex web of distinctions among the network of elements that constitute a literary work is necessary, even though I intend to stress the interplay and interrelationships that exist among them. The distinctions are necessary because when critics allude to the "conventionality" of the pastoral genre, it is rarely clear to what aspect or element in the literary unit that constitutes a work they are referring. Thus when a contemporary Spanish critic says: "Nadie vio en las

---

(14) Greg, for instance, follows three broad categories as conventional: allegorical, realistic, and escapist. W. W. Greg, *op. cit.*, p. 7. Poggioli, expanding from these general groups classifies all levels and variations of possible pastoral subjects. See Renato Poggioli, *The Oaten Flute*, Cambridge, Harvard University Press, 1976.

convenciones pastoriles, dioses, peligro alguno para el dogma" (15) convention is taken as the use of pagan deities, nymphs and characters that had been commonplace in Classical Antiquity. When another critic says "Gallus is *conventionally* represented as surrounded by Arcadian shepherds who listen to his plaintive song of unrequited love" (16), he is referring to the thematic setting as the general meaning of conventionality.

Thus the examination of the arguments regarding the concept of convention itself had to take priority in the development of my analysis. However because some of the main characteristics associated with the concept of convention in the study of literature are also shared by other concepts and theories of undeniable importance, I found it necessary to clarify the interrelationship between convention and other concepts. This is the subject of the following section.

Concepts Relevant to the Study of Conventions: the Dominant, the topoi, Imitation and Influence

The purpose of this section is to build upon the previous discussion of conventions by differentiating the term "convention" from other terms and concepts having a semantic or structural relationship with it. While the discussion necessarily involves consideration of macro- and micro-contexts, an emphasis on macro-contexts will predominate here. Specifically emphasis will be placed on the concept of the *dominant* in the Jakobsonian sense of the term; the concept of *topos*, i.e. the theory of culturally shared commonplaces

---

(15) Marcial José Bayo, *Virgilio y la Pastoril española del Renacimiento (1480-1530)*, Madrid, Gredos, 1959, p. 99.
(16) W. Leonard Grant, *op. cit.*, p. 70.

elaborated by E. R. Curtius (17); and the concepts of imitation and influence as they relate to Renaissance aesthetics, particularly in the relationship between Aristotelian and neo-platonic aesthetics.

As previously mentioned, a number of key features are implied in uses of the word *convention*. In discussing the application of the term to macro-contexts, the most significant characteristics (in addition to implicit consensus) are coherence or integratory quality, durability, and transferability. These characteristics have been studied in relation to a variety of fields, e.g. philosophy, social theory, literature. In literature, they have been examined in connection with the theory of the "dominant," and the theories of the *topoi* and permanence of their cultural elements (18), and with theories of imitation and influence.

Given the undeniable value of these theories for understanding the problems of literary art and their close relation to concepts like convention, it is necessary to discuss them in relation to conventions, and to point out the similarities and differences between them.

The Theory of the "Dominant"

As already mentioned in the earlier definition of the term convention, there is an implicit emphasis in it on a significant cohesive character. The integratory quality of the convention is not only derived from the role of conventions as part of larger systems or contexts, but because they are capable of imparting homogeneity and cohesion to them. In literature, these agreements, examined at the most general level, could serve as indicators of the style and aims of a given period,

---

(17) Ernst R. Curtius, *European Literature and the Latin Middle Ages*, translator W. Trask, Princeton, Princeton University Press, 1953.

(18) Jean Seznec, *The Survival of the Pagan Gods*, translator, B. F. Sessions, New York, Harper Torchbooks, 1953.

group, or artistic school. Seen on a more reduced scale, they aid our understanding and appreciation of different literary genres, modes, and individual works of art.

In recent literary studies, this integrative, focusing component has been brought to general attention by Roman Jakobson in specific relation to the elements of versification in his theory of the *dominant*. Jakobson defines this concept as:

> *The focusing component of a work of art: it rules, determines and transforms the remaining components. It is the dominant which guarantees the integrity of the structure.* (19)

He states that in the language of verse—which is a hierarchical system of values—, the dominant is the leading value ". . . without which (within the framework of a given literary period and a given artistic trend) verse cannot be conceived and evaluated as verse" (20).

Expanded to literature in general, this formalist theory takes a view of literary evolution in which elements interact within a system with continual shifting among the different components. What matters for the idea of the dominant is not what elements prevail or disappear in an absolute sense. Rather the center of attention is ". . . the question of the shifting dominant" (21), the moving balance of dominant elements. The formalists' main concern is to stress the shifts, deviations and changes these elements undergo.

This specialized concept of the "dominant" is of use for the present study because there is an analogy between the

---

(19) Roman Jakobson, "The Dominant" in *Readings in Russian Poetics: Formalist and Structural Views*, L. Matejka and K. Pomovska, eds., Cambridge, Mass., M.I.T. Press, 1971, pp. 82-87.

(20) *Ibid.*, p. 82.

(21) *Ibid.*, p. 82.

role of the dominant and the use of pastoral language. The "dominant" structures the poetic space in a way that is analogous to the use of controlled pastoral language to create specific coherence among the linguistic forms and thematic elements in pastoral works.

As in any genre, including pastoral, there is, however, change in the agreements or conventions. Certain conventions enjoy a durability extending beyond the mere elaboration and use by a particular author or literary school. And conventions seem to lose their efficacy after some time, becoming static and finally disappearing from the literary mainstream while others, after many adaptations and changes, are replaced by other conventions better fitted to new tastes or aesthetic demands resulting from a new "dominant" aesthetic view.

We have one such example of this evolutionary shift in the reverse simile of the column and the tree. This literary trope can be traced to its first literary appearance in Ovid's Story of Cyparissus (22). In accordance with the allegorical ethos of Ovidian aesthetics, the young shepherd of the gods is transformed by Apollo into a cypress tree, a symbol of mourning. The allegory of mourning and the symbolic tree were widely used through the Middle Ages (23) and were recovered again many times by Boccaccio, among others, to fit the stylistic demands of his pastoral themes (24). It is more pronounced in Boccaccio largely because he relied very directly on allegorical figures for his themes.

The consensus regarding this transformation up to the Renaissance seemed to have demanded an allegorical mechanism that placed nature (the youth in this case, i.e. human nature) within nature (the cypress tree, i.e. botannical nature)

---

(22) Ovid, *Metamorphoses*, 10: 106-42.

(23) The success of Pierre Bersuire's *Ovide moralisé* (ca. 1340) attests to this. Cf. Jean Seznec, *op. cit.*, especially Part II, I: "The Metamorphoses of the Gods," pp. 149-183.

(24) Boccaccio, *Il Ninfale Fiesolano* (first published in 1477 although written much earlier).

in metaphorical relationship. Time and again the transformations worked in this fashion. Then in Sanazzaro's *Arcadia* (ca. 1504), there is a departure from the analogy person/tree that had prevailed for so long as a theme favored in pastoral works, as well as in other genres. Right at the beginning of his book, we find the same image, although this time greatly transformed: ". . . in their midst, near a limpid fountain, soaring toward heaven a straight cypress, a most *accurate imitator of the lofty obelisks*" (25). Following a definitely new view where art is on an equal footing with nature, Sanazzaro presents the natural elements as imitators of man-made artifice.

My point here is that a new macro-contextual convention, i.e., the view of art as a powerful instrument, made possible the reversal and appreciation of a new twist in the nature/man metaphor.

This is one of the many examples in Renaissance aesthetics where the idea of nature imitating art, and even art imitating art as in this case, is explored and illustrated. It became one of the predominant concerns, a "dominant" in the sense of commonly shared, as a concept repeatedly discussed in pastoral works. These reversed metamorphoses cultivated in the Renaissance became a most important element in Baroque and mannerist aesthetics. However, after an endless series of adaptations and usages, they, in turn, became dated, being identified with the elaborate rhetorical figures characteristic of these schools, and finally they disappeared with the new demands of Neoclassical aesthetics.

---

(25) Jacopo Sanazzaro, also spelled Sannazaro and Sannazzaro, *Arcadia & Piscatorial Eclogues*, translator Ralph Nash, Detroit, Wayne State University Press, 1966, I, p. 31.

The *topoi*

Closely related to the above approach to the popularity, acceptance, and continuous adaptation of particular themes, concepts, and rhetorical forms is a phenomenon systematized by E. R. Curtius in his theory of the *topoi*. He considers the *topoi* as primary units that travel through literature but which remain traceable and permanent as units (26). More recently, René Wellek has defined them as "Commonplaces . . . recurrent themes and images which are handed down from Antiquity through the Latin Middle Ages and permeate all modern literature" (27). In both definitions, the character of endurance, inherent in the *topoi*, is directly related to the problems of continuity and change in literary history.

Curtius' own aim, however, is to formulate a unified theory of European ideas of which literary *topoi* are a sort of repository, a "thesaurus" of permanent elements. I do not accept this view in regard to conventions, even with recognizable themes that have been used repeatedly over the ages in European letters. The agreements or model consensus that gain general importance at any given time must be based upon interpretation. Cultural traditions cannot be usefully seen as static building blocks to be combined and recombined. Rather they are repertoires of possibilities (28). The very act

---

(26) Ernst R. Curtius, *op. cit.*, see pp. 82 and ff.

(27) René Wellek and Austin Warren, *Theory of Literature*, New York, Harcourt, Brace and Co., 1956, p. 249. See also René Wellek, *The Concept of Criticism*, New Haven, Yale University Press, 1963, p. 20.

(28) Seznec, in his book (*op. cit.*) comments on the concept of resurfacing, the reappearance of figures, Gods, and myths of the Classical past saying: "The preceding study [of figures] . . . authorize[s] us to define more exactly, or to rectify, certain ideas and terms—first of all, the very notion of 'Renaissance' itself. . . . Not for a moment is there any question of 'resurrection'; Hercules had never died, any more than Mars or Perseus. As concepts and as names, at least, they had survived tenaciously in the memory of man. It was their appearance alone which

of taking up one of the possibilities involves an artistic (definitely purposeful) transformation of the pre-existing form in which its link to the past and its essential uniqueness must both be recognized.

I will take up one example. In studying a very durable theme in Western literature, the *topos* of the pleasance or *locus amoenus*, following Curtius' systematic analysis, we find, in passages where this *topos* occurs, a detailed description of elements of exotic flora—willows, birch trees, olive and palm groves—and sometimes equally exotic fauna. These contribute to the ideal beauty of the *loci*. Curtius links together a chronological description of those enchanting landscapes from Greek (Theocritus) to medieval (Ekkehan IV of St Gall) to Shakespeare, and to Goethe (29), as they proceed in a continuous literary tradition to contemporary works. He then traces the etymological, rhetorical, and morphological aspects of the works under study to end with an analytical discussion.

What follows from his method is that the *topoi* endured; they were *necessarily* adopted because they are part of the "thesaurus." This does not explain why some themes are chosen over other similar or better ones; nor does it take into account the variety of, and often contradictory reasons that condition the adoption of a given *topos*. Thus the endurance of the *topos* has been conveniently attributed to a view of influence that sees literary tradition as a linear, inexorable current rather than as an activity involving acts of interpretation and selection.

The study of literary history suggests that there is no direct sequence from time period to time period. There are and have been ideas, philosophies, themes that caught the mind and spirit of people for a long time. Occasionally these seem

---

had vanished, Perseus living on in his Turkish disguise and Mars as a knight of chivalry," p. 211.

(29) Ernst R. Curtius, *op. cit.*, p. 183.

to be intensified by the special impact of an important author, a genial work, or an extraordinary event. But this does not preclude the existence and co-existence of equally appealing and influential ideas which can be and often are in total contradiction with the other one.

Just which elements will be carried on in continuing adaptations of combinations of previously accepted ideas cannot be predicted. Yet, the concepts of influence and imitation have been generally taken as referring to just such a predetermined direct linear passage.

Influence and Imitation

Probably since literature became clearly established as a powerful and specialized human activity, there has been a debate about the impact of imitation and influence as compared with artistic originality or creativity (30). The issue centers on the human problem of simultaneously being part of a tradition and experiencing the need or impulse to break with that tradition. This longstanding debate has waxed hot, especially when the agreements or rules within which literary works were produced were held to be rigidly binding.

In the Spanish Golden Age, for instance, this particular issue became an arena of competition among schools, theories, and authors. The contest was between the so-called *preceptistas* (those following strictly Aristotelian and Horacian rules) and those who advocated total independence. When the argument is formulated in this extreme way the role of the artist, his interpretative abilities and artistic awareness are neglected.

In recent years, there has been a shift in emphasis and the role of the author comes to the forefront. In Foucault, for

---

(30) One of the earliest and better documented examples in this regard is Plato's pronouncement against the vices of rhetoricians. On the subject of imitation one should, of course, consult Aristotle's *Poetics*.

instance, it is the "privileged authors," those who lead the revolt against rigid artistic norms and authoritarian figures, who will create truly new experiences (31).

While I will not deny the value and importance of this view of the role of the author as innovator, I do wish to focus attention on another point: working within well-defined and understood aesthetic principles does not necessarily imply a lack of originality. A great author is always an interpreter (of experience, of behavior, of other texts) and as such, an active participant who may, indeed must, modify the material he works with.

That it is necessary to work within certain rules, especially when attempting to answer the questions generated within a particular world-view, is simply to repeat a sort of cliché, a truism: art does not come from nowhere. A truly great artist is the one who relates most cogently to the great art already in existence. Indeed, even Foucault's view presupposes this previous existence, though he stresses a total break with the existing epistemes, radical discontinuity as constituting different periods (32).

Pastoral works illustrate the need for this dual emphasis in a most striking way. These narratives are definitely conventional in forms, themes, and structure: yet a consistent feature of pastoral, stressed by numerous commentators and scholars, is the innovation found in each of the major works, their difference from previous works in the same pastoral narrative tradition.

W. W. Greg, comments that Virgil had changed the character of the eclogues by departing from the way Theocritus treated the physical environment (33). Theocritus in turn,

---

(31) Michel Foucault, *Language, Countermeaning and Practice*, translator, D. Bouchard, Ithaca, Cornell University Press, 1977, p. 21.

(32) Michel Foucault, *The Order of Things*, New York, Vintage, 1973.

(33) W. W. Greg, *Pastoral Poetry and Pastoral Drama*, London, A.H. Bullen, 1906, p. 13.

had refined the style and themes of the pre-Hellenistic poets in his adaptations of form and style (34).

In sum, the masters of pastoral are also those who interpret and elaborate, adapting the material they work with into a more effective expression. To do this, they imitate and copy recognized masters of earlier times as well as their own contemporary counterparts. Indeed, this adaptation and copying became in the Renaissance part of a convention: proof of their training as humanists and a demonstration of their artistry.

In the case of Renaissance pastoral works, these issues are also related to the rediscovery of Aristotelian aesthetic principles and their overall impact on cultural and artistic movements.

The followers of the Aristotelian "mimesis" based these imitative processes on naturalistic foundations. The Spanish humanist, Alfonso Sanchez summed this up:

We have art, we have precepts and rules which bind us, and the principal precept is to imitate nature, for the works of poets express the nature, the manners, and the genius of the age in which they write. (35)

Yet coexisting with the interpretations and practice of Aristotelian aesthetics, there was a Neoplatonic perspective, with special emphasis on the role of inspiration, the cult of beauty and of love. It took an equally strong hold in the ideas and works of authors of the same countries and the same historical periods.

Together the Aristotelian principles of "verisimilitude" (coherence between Nature and the ways of art) and the neo-

---

(34) G. M. Kirkwood, *Early Greek Monody*, Ithaca, Cornell University Press, 1976.

(35) Cited by M. Menendez y Pelayo, *Historia de las ideas estéticas en España*, segunda edición, 9 vols., Madrid, 1890-1896 but quoted and translated by J. E. Spingarn, *op. cit.*, p. 234.

platonic view of art (36) gave rise to innovations, stressing the importance of the national traditions, with their roots in popular and church versions of the medieval theater, and related arts.

Artists of the late Renaissance, Cervantes and the poets in Spain for instance, synthesized converging currents and created a new approach to art that revolutionized Spanish literature forever. What Cervantes accomplished had the most enriching effects on literary narratives and the literary arts in general. A similar effort and accomplishment took place through the concerted activities of groups such as la Pléiade in France.

What must be stressed is that these authors' successes were in agreement, were *vraisemblable*, within the newly accepted context of rhetorical rules, the newly adapted concepts of the imaginal in art, and with cultivation of indigenous national traditional forms as sources of inspiration. Indeed this macro-contextual aspect of agreements and rules that enable new forms to exist and to succeed must lie at the center of the whole study of pastoral.

Conclusions

To review, this discussion of the different usages and meanings related to the term convention is not intended to be

---

(36) The neoplatonic concepts as interpreted by León Hebreo in *Diálogos de Amor* (1542) enjoyed a tremendous success in Spain for instance and his ideas permeated the peninsular pastoral. Petrus Ramus introduced the neoplatonic doctrines in le Collège de France (1536) and Giordano Bruno traveled to England proposing a change from Aristotelianism in favor of the Neoplatonic views. See J. E. Spingarn, *A History of Literary Criticism in the Renaissance*, New York, Columbia University Press, 1908, p. 227.

either exhaustive or complete. Rather I aimed first to stress the importance of understanding conventions in the literary enterprise and to show how they are constitutive elements—micro-contexts within a general system of values and communication—at the same time they are the macro-contexts where the cultural, authorial, intratextual, and intertextual relationships occur.

Pastoral aesthetics, relying so heavily on rhetorical artifice stresses the role of eloquence, beauty, eurhythm in art. In its remoteness from the determinacy of the "real" in the empirical sense, it provides another kind of reality, a reminder that human activity and creativity also exists at a level clearly different from the empirical.

The qualities of coherence and endurance, though shared with the concepts of the dominant and the *topoi*, are most centrally associated with the concept of convention. Thus although ordinary usage seems to indicate otherwise, the qualities of transmutability and adaptation are intimately associated with the concept of convention, as it is applied in the poetics of pastoral: indeed they are implied by it. For these reasons, repeated vague references to the conventionality of the pastoral genre are extremely misleading. They not only misrepresent the genre and ultimately eliminate our hopes of ever understanding it, but they also rest on a fundamental misunderstanding of the concept of literary convention itself.

CHAPTER III

PASTORAL AND THE PROMOTION OF LITERARY ART

The use of these literary conventions in these pastoral works helps us to understand how fictional worlds are created and epitomizes the human importance of the world of the imagination, a world as crucial to use as the everyday realm of reality. An excursion into the fictional pastoral world provides the audience with new ways of discovering meaning in their sentimental experiences, providing powerful analogies for understanding what is behind more immediately empirical experiences.

This cosmopolitan literature places great emphasis on the equilibrium among all the constitutive elements, making pastoral both remote and unique. This attention to harmonious perfection is one of the many consequences derived from the awareness of art and its power. Awareness of the powers of artistic language, in particular, is manifested with great profusion in a variety of literary works in the Renaissance. Particularly striking here is the awareness of language as an instrument, a multifunctional, multipurpose tool. In this, pastoral is simply part of broader developments.

This phenomenon, so acute in the Renaissance, is not exclusively restricted to that period (1). From the famous Platonic objections to the use and abuse of rhetoric to the arguments about Ciceronian versus Asiatic styles to the medieval debates (Isidore of Seville in the sixth century, John of Salisbury in the twelfth, to Dante in the fourteenth, and so on), the question has remained alive right up to the present time, including recent, extensive studies of language and linguistic science (2). Many of the issues related to this interest is language centered around questions still hotly debated. Some of them were squarely confronted in the major pastoral narratives of the Renaissance. In particular the pastorals dealt with two issues. First, what are the characteristics that differentiate literary art from the non-artistic usage of language, and second, within artistic usage, what are the appropriate vehicles of artistic expressivity.

In confronting these questions, the authors of pastoral show clear sense of their artistic intent which, as they themselves state, is to promote a new, more refined kind of literary art. This purpose was perhaps best expressed by Virgil in his *Eclogues*, though, as I will discuss later, this awareness of literary art was by then already an established intentional agreement, a convention of the genre.

---

(1) For a reassessment of these issues see W. Leonard Grant, *Neo-Latin Literature and the Pastoral*, Chapel Hill, The Univeristy of North Carolina Press, 1965; Nancy Steuver, *The Language of History in the Renaissance*, Princeton, Princeton University Press, 1970; and Paolo Valesio, *Novantiqua*, Bloomington, Indiana University Press, 1980.

(2) The number of studies on these subjects as they apply to literary language is enormous. The bibliography alone could occupy a thesis. Some of the collections of papers that I found particularly relevant include William O. Hendricks, *Essays on Semiolinguistics and Verbal Art*, The Hague, Mouton, 1973 and L. Matejka and J. R. Titunik, *Semiotics of Art: Prague School Contributions*, Cambridge, Mass., The MIT Press, 1976.

Virgil states:

Non omnes arbusta iuvant humilesque myricae;
si canimus silvas, silvae sint consule dignae (Eclogue 4, 2-3)

It is a conscious, concerted effort aimed at a refined, cultivated audience. Authors' attitudes toward this task and the explanation of their purposes is not uniform. As would be expected given the differences in time, country, and personal situation, statements from different authors reflect attitudes that range from marked uneasiness to enthusiastic admission of the artistic purposes in their work.

Thus, for instance, Honoré d'Urfé confidently explains the reasons for his selected mode of refined expression at the beginning of *L'Astrée* (3):

Que si vos conceptions et paroles estoient veritablement telles que celles des Bergers ordinaires, ils aurient aussi peu de plaisir de vous escouter que vous auriez beaucoup de honte à les redire. (L'autheur a la Bergère Astrée)

In apparent contrast with that view, Sanazzaro faced the question of artistic expression with a commitment to a cultivation of simplicity in the famous "A la sampogna," the epilogue to his *Arcadia:*

Per la qual cosa io ti prego e quanto posso ti ammonisco, che della tua salvatichezza contentandoti, tra queste solitudine ti rimanghi. . . . Nè ti curare, se alcuno, usato forse di udire più esquisiti suoni, con ischifo gusto schernisse la tua bassezza, o ti chiamasse rozza: che veramente, se ben

---

(3) The majority of references to *L'Astrée* will be taken from the most recent abridged edition which is *L'Astrée* [*prècédé de La serpent dans la bergerie*], Gèrard Genette, ed., Paris, Union Générale d'éditions, 1964. Others from the edition of Hugues Vaganay, Lyon, P. Masson, 1925.

pensi, questa è la tua propria e principalissima lode; purchè
da' boschi, e da' luoghi a te conveniente non ti departa. (4)

The discussion of lowness and rusticity is, as I show later, an ironic one.

Cervantes, equally concerned with the problems involved in the rhetorical ornamentation for the accurate, appropriate expression of intense feelings, puts the following words into one of the shepherds complaints in *La Galatea:*

Orfinio:
   . . .
comience el que quisiere
y dé a los otros muestra
de su dolor con torpe lengua o diestra:
     que no está en la elegancia
y modo de decir el fundamento
y principal sustancia
del verdadero cuento
que en la pura verdad tiene su asiento. (5)

In this view, the substance of a story is found not in elegant ornamentation but in its pure truth. This substance, as discussed by Cervantes throughout his work (6), includes literary truth. The implications derived from these assertions will be dealt with in later chapters. My point here is to underline Cervantes' undeniable artistic awareness when he expounds the choice between the rustic and sophisticated language as means of expression in art.

---

(4) Jacopo Sanazzaro, *Arcadia*, Luigi Portirelli, ed., Milano, Societá Tipografica de' Classici Italiani, 1806, pp. 211, 213.
(5) Miguel de Cervantes, *La Galatea*, Madrid, Clásicos castellanos, Espasa-Calpe, 1968, book III, pp. 215-216.
(6) For a thorough discussion of this point, see E. C. Riley, *Cervantes's Theory of the Novel*, Oxford, Oxford University Press, 1962, p. 84 and ff.

Whether in clear confidence or explicit ambivalence, the authors of pastoral works, as they explain, are deeply concerned with the artistic manipulation of language, the refined mediation through which the ordinary and common is transformed and the lofty, difficult, and recondite is expressed. This is done in a purposeful and contrived way that was to become the trademark and has been the "convention" since the first documented pastoral works in the Hellenistic period.

Thus Anthony Holden, in his translation of the Greek *Idylls*, comments that the achievement of the Hellenistic poets was in fact a concerted élitist one ". . . which sought to raise the dwindling quality of Greek literature by treating the best-known local folklore and legends in the most refined and intellectual literary terms" (7). This argument could be directly applied to Theocritus of Syracuse who, around the year 270 B.C. became part of the school of poetry on the island of Cos (Kos). It would also undoubtedly apply to Bion and Muschus who, about a century after him, continued his poetic innovations (8). We will see a number of authors who followed this in the creation of particular literary expressions.

The Eclogues and the Idylls

A wealth of scholarship in the best tradition has been dedicated to Theocritus and Virgil. The analysis devoted to the similarities and differences in the function of nature in their

---

(7) Anthony Holden, *Greek Pastoral Poetry*, Harmondsworth, Middlesex, Penguin Books, 1974, p. 13.

(8) Bion, best known for his Idyll "Woe, woe for Adonis" is placed by some authorities around one hundred years after Theocritus. Moschus, a Sicilian, probably wrote about 150 B.C. His most important extant work is his "Lament for Bion." See Anthony Holden, *op. cit., loc. cit.*

idyllic and pastoral worlds is of central interest here. Relevant also are studies concerning the relation of these masters' poetic themes and techniques to the politics of their respective times. For my purposes, I concentrate primarily on one aspect of this work: their efforts as conscious, dedicated artists intellectually involved in creating a definite poetics. I am not, however, dealing here with the problems of the "artist engagé" although this is a clear and important aspect of their role, nor am I analyzing this subject from the viewpoint of problems of influence. Theocritus' *Idylls* and Virgil's entire corpus demonstrate both their awareness of their artistic task and the role of the artist as one of the major elements in the development of a culture.

Idylls

Let us begin with the background and intentional considerations in Theocritus' *Idylls*. The *idylls*—little pictures decribing selected episodes of country life in a blend of Doric dialects and stylized, poetically elaborated expressions—were themselves assimilated versions and adaptations of works produced at the above-mentioned school by Philitas, Sophron and others.

What was then a new blend of forms and themes in traditional as well as in new elegant terms was achieved by Theocritus in his *Idylls*. Modern critics such as Holden, in this regard, consider Idyll I: "Tyrsis' Lament for Daphnis," Idyll III: "The Serenade," and Idyll VII: "The Harvest Feast" and Idyll XI: "The Cyclops" among the best representations of this successful mixture.

Some lines from Idyll XI: "The Cyclops" will help to illustrate:

There's nothing else, Nicias, no other cure
for love; no other antidote, I say, no salve:

only the Muses. Theirs is a gentle remedy,
relieving mortal pain—yet not easy to find.
But you know this, I think, you know it well,
being a doctor, and indeed one they much love.
It's how the Cyclops, my countryman, found comfort
in his love for Galatea. Polyphemus, so the old story goes,

. . . . .
He nursed deep in his breast an angry wound,
a pain in his heart from great Cypris' bow.
Yet he found this cure; and he'd sit on a rock,
high up, looking out to sea, and would sing: (9)

The evocative mixture of poetic skills—the "gentle remedy" but also the difficult gift of the Muses—and the genuine knowledge and delight in nature and rural ways was to become conventional for later pastoral works. The convention applies both to the macro-contextual sense of awareness of poetic language and specialized efforts for the poets, and to the micro-contextual expressions of themes, settings, and forms.

The laudatory initial address to a fellow poet is indicative of the elite *communitas* involved in the poetic arts. Nicias is an insider, and as thus, able to appreciate the difficulties and the rewards of poetry. He also understands the meaning of the mythological allusions, personal hints, and the arrangement of the folk ("old story") integrated into a poeticized new "little picture," the idyll. The speaker addresses the poem to him because the Doctor is familiar with the art.

This idyll's micro-contextual expressions of world-weariness and love wounds cured by the poetic sources found in nature appeared in most other idylls as well. Thus, for instance, we find it in Moschus when he writes:

_____

(9) Anthony Holden, *op. cit.*, pp. 88-89.

*Would that my father had taught me the craft of a keeper
of sheep,
for so in the shade of the elm-tree, or under the rocks on
the steep
Piping on the reeds I had set, and had lulled my sorrows to
sleep.* (10)

Though the thematic evocation of pastoral bliss by the sentimental shepherd has been considered one of the most typical characteristics of the conventional pastoral, particularly of pastoral poetry and romances, I would stress that the possibilities contained in the specialized, elaborated concrete units constituting each idyll whether they are expressed in poetic compositions, in prose narratives or in dramatic forms or the structural arrangement of singing matches between shepherds, hymns, dirges, and praises of patrons in episodic tableaux include far more than mere thematic derivations.

The choice of the idyll form and the interweaving of these themes is but one of the many responses to the problems that the poetic endeavor poses to the artist. This particular response—the idyll format—permits a particular kind of elaboration that presents a positive mirror or model where those poetic problems are confronted and solutions found.

Further, the positive, beautiful model is especially important because certain problems and events do not seem to be noticed or appreciated unless they have been placed in a most enhancing light. Just as we notice things when they come upon us in a shocking way, so we perceive problems, aspects of things, and events when we see them in isolation, selected and presented in a separate and especially beautiful way. The potential impact of the idyll is great since it is particularly suited to such presentations.

---

(10) A fragment, translated by Ernest Myers, as quoted by W. W. Greg in his *Pastoral Poetry and Pastoral Drama*, London, A. H. Bullen, 1906, p. 11.

Given the variety of possibilities, the choice of format by the pastoral authors is not accidental. It is clearly a well thought out decision, as the very names of the compositions indicates (11).

Another important element is the way pastoral compositions integrate the familiar sounds and themes of folk poetry into a new, sophisticated format that was itself accepted and came to be an enduring part of the tradition. For instance, the new Theocritan version of the old Cyclops myth with its particular combination of the familiar with the unfamiliar artifice emphasizes the importance of poetic art.

This aspect of literature has received deserved attention recently, centering on the study of the value of what is familiar and the commonplaces as elements of expressivity. Although these studies are perhaps more numerous with regard to language in general [proverbs (12), emblems (13), and clichés in non-artistic speech (e.g. McLuhan)], a few studies concentrate on the role that these fixed, common expressions play in literature (e.g. McLuhan, 1970, Riffaterre, 1964, Holdheim, 1978).

---

(11) Scholars of this subject have commented on this point. E. R. Curtius, for instance, says about the choice of names for the compositions: "Virgil's pastoral poems (*Bucolica*) consists of ten 'eclogues'. *Ecloga* means 'selected composition', but later becomes the generic term for pastoral poetry." In *European Literature and the Latin Middle Ages*, Princeton, Princeton University Press, 1953, p. 190, note 13.

(12) Wolfgang Mieder, "The Use of Proverbs," *The Journal of American Folklore*, Vol. 91, Fall 1978:45-54; G. L. Permyakov, *From Proverbs to Folk-Tale: Notes on the General Theory of the Cliché*, Bloomington, Indiana University Press, 1976.

(13) Studies of emblems since the Renaissance have been based on the original Latin version *Emblemata* by the Venetian Andrea Alciati (1531). Recent interpretations include Milton Klonsky, *Speaking Pictures*, Harmony Books, 1977 and D. J. Gordon, *The Renaissance Imagination: Essays and Lectures*, Berkeley, University of California Press, 1977. Cf. John Hollander, "Talkies" in *The New York Review of Books*, December 8, 1977: 50-54.

Riffaterre (14), for instance, does not see the clichés or fixed expressions of language as an indication of weakness or style altogether devoid of originality and possibilities of interpretation. Rather he considers these clichés as expressive linguistic units. While he is exclusively concerned with the stylistic field that those clichés create within a given text, my attention is drawn to this because the pastoral authors often use commonplace expressions that eventually come to be used in all the texts of the genre. They are repeated from work to work thus creating an intertextual field. Rather than resulting in a vulgarization, the cliché pastoral forms, if inserted in the texts with art and skill, can be at once assimilated and yet remain special.

Returning to more general considerations now, the structure of singing matches that revolved around the themes of shared love, unrequited love, death, and the praise of patrons occurring against a stage-like immutable landscape were the frames within which the questions of the defense of the poetic art and its aims and the praise of poetry itself were developed in pastoral. Their structuring as a mixture of formal elements (the match, the complaint, the hymn, etc.) in episodic segments and as thematic concerns expressed in the most elegant forms (at times together with "rustic" expressions) provide needed flexibility of adaptation and the opportunity for specialized treatment of any one of the thematic concerns. This mixture of elements reappears in adapted form in other genres as well and, of course, it is also indiscriminately considered as a conventional feature of pastoral. Expanded versions and adaptations of these "little pictures" were later to be found, not only in idylls, but in eclogues, romances, and dramatized versions (15) whose roots can be

---

(14) Michael Riffaterre, "La Fonction du cliché dans la prose littèraire," *CAIEF*; Paris, Vol. 16 (1946):82-83.

(15) A detailed documentation of the derivations of drama is found in W. W. Greg, *op. cit.*, especially Chapter III "Italian Drama," Chapter IV "Dramatic Origins" and Chapter VII "Masques." For a more recent

traced to the "idyllic" descriptions and episodes of the earlier compositions of the Greek poets.

Thus there is a durability of the thematic convention in such diverse works and times in the concern with beautiful expression, elaborations on the questions of human feeling, and the need to retreat to an unspoiled milieu as the only way to find that which is genuine. All these seem to find the best literary vehicle in the enlarged idyll and the use of euphemic devices.

There is also a great effectiveness in combining the artificiality and refinement of forms with evocative spontaneity often found in folk art and themes. This combination requires wit and command of literary skills, and is often employed by authors to display their art.

It is an understatement to say that the efforts of Theocritus and his followers were successful. The achievements of these poets are proof of their personal genius. But the establishment of this particular poetic form, the idyll, was also the result of concerted intellectual and cultural efforts similar to those undertaken by artists and thinkers of other periods in history. Central to their success was their ability to combine such a complex array of forms (odes), structures (singing match) and thematic elements (love complaints) in one genre.

Eclogues

Despite the label of conventionality the pastoral moved in more than one direction. Along with the romance, the *Eclogue* is the most widely known form derived from the early idylls, which in turn proved to be adaptable to all sorts of literary expressions from the sentimental to the political, from the lyric to the dramatic, from the panegyric to the

---

treatment of the subject as it developed in the Neo-Latin works of the early Renaissance, see W. Leonard Grant, *op. cit.*

parodic (16). Because of their conciseness and flexible character, they provide a special kind of unity where full vignettes, themes and episodes can be developed. Although not all pastorals are in the form of eclogues, the aside-like songs, the segments, the "nested" story-within-story composition of the structure of the romances, makes full use of the eclogue concept. In other words, in addition to the independent song-unit eclogue as it appeared in classical works, the concept itself was adapted in the romances for other uses. There were eclogues proper in the texts, but they, and other eclogue-like units, were inserted as concrete units; that is stories that can be stopped, interwoven and compartmentalized. In this sense the eclogue concept is another example of re-adaptation from an earlier form.

Virgil, who around the year 30 B.C. was part of an intellectual and artistic movement taking place in concert with political changes in imperial Rome, re-elaborated those forms of lyric Greek literature in his ten *Eclogues* or *Bucolics*. He, perhaps more than any other poet, contributed to the establishment (conventionalization) of this particular mode of artistic expression. He renamed his poetic compositions dealing with pastoral themes as "eclogues" from the Greek ex logos which means "out of the discourse," and also selection or excerpt. The eclogues are, thus, re-elaborations of previous modes of expression, the *Idylls*.

One form that was repeatedly cultivated from the first dialogic amoebean debates of the Theocritan shepherds through the medieval "pastoureles" is the pastoral drama. One of the first important Renaissance pastorals was in fact a "mime,"

_____

(16) Many studies would be relevant to this subject. In addition to the works of Grant, Greg and Curtius, already cited, the most thorough classification of all modes of pastoral is probably Renato Poggioli's *The Oaten Flute*, Cambridge, Harvard University Press, 1975. Also for the application of several pastoral themes to the theater, cf. Georges Hérelle, *Representations Pastorales à sujets tragiques*, Paris, 1923.

patterned after the dialogues of the Idylls and perhaps after the IX Eclogue, *Tirsi*. I say *Tirsi* because it may well have been this dramatic eclogue that Castiglione accompanied by Cesare Gonzaga, revived in the year 1506 (17) before the court of the Duke Guidubaldo at Urbino. This eclogue begins with the simple pastoral complaints and ends with a political panegyric on the court and members of the court in the manner of *Il Cortegiano*. Thus romances and eclogues themselves are examples of repetition and renewal.

Just as important as the transmission of the genre itself and certain forms are the repetition and renewal of specific linguistic conventions. To them I now turn.

Specific Linguistic Conventions

An early example of the cultivation of pre-selected, already known literary forms (in the sense that they already exist in literary texts) is the Theocritan use of Homeric characters and names such as Polyphemus (*The Odyssey*, Book IX; "The Cyclops"). Around the theme of the ugly, monstrous giant, Theocritus worked the theme of unrequited love for the traditional, legendary nymph Galatea (who in turn belonged to a body of folk stories of unknown authorship).

A few centuries later, Virgil, involved in a similar artistic quest, selected the same names and the same themes for his Eighth Eclogue (39 B.C.). In this case, however, the contrast between Beauty and Beast is not the only or the main concern. Virgil stressed the almost perfect reproduction of a particular situation: the precise moment when the speaker remembers his first encounter with his beloved and his ensu-

---

(17) Cf. Greg, *op. cit.*, p. 31.

ing surrender to love. This remembrance is told in terms almost identical to those used by Theocritus:

I have loved you, lady, since you first came
with your mother,
to pick hyacinths on my hill.
I showed you the way. And since that hour,
since I saw you, my love has not changed.

Theocritus, Idyll XII "The Cyclops," 25-29 (18)

When you were small I saw you (I was then your guide)
with your mother
picking the dewy apples in our orchard
I had just entered the year after my eleventh year;
already I could touch the delicate branches from the
  ground
I saw you and, Ah, was lost;
this wicked treachery of love caught me.

Virgil, Eclogue VIII, 37-41 (19)

The reproduction of themes is clear—Homer is re-elaborated by Theocritus who is in turn repeated by Virgil. It seems fundamental to understand the awareness and determination of the authors to reproduce the names, situations, and words already used in other well-known works. The repetition of names, expressions, and even the literal copying of complete verses and stanzas belonging to earlier pastoral compositions of famous authors either from classical literature or from masters of their own vernacular languages who in turn derived them from classical literatures—e.g. Boccaccio, Sanazzaro, Boscan, Cervantes, and Spenser is one of the

---

(18) Anthony Holden, translation, *op. cit.*, pp. 88-89.
(19) Laurence Lerner, translator, in *The Uses of Nostalgia: Studies in Pastoral Poetry*, London, Chatto and Windus, 1972, p. 61.

most identifiable formal "conventions" in the pastoral narratives of the Renaissance. This practice, which has been
studied by critics largely concerned with the questions of
imitation and influence is of great relevance to the aesthetics
of pastoral. I deem it important to stress the intertextual relationships cultivated by the followers of this literature (20),
as well as the inner coherence of all the literary elements that
this genre aims to achieve.

This cultivation and revival of literary formulae involves a
clear understanding of the artistic enterprise as something
other than an isolated, de-contextualized human operation.
Indeed, it points to the necessary hermeneutical activities
that constitute the basis of human culture.

As the examples of Theocritus' idyll and Virgil's eclogue illustrate, there are a number of common experiences that are
best understood and shared when expressed in a similar way,
when recalled (almost literally in this case) with the same
words (21). In the concrete case of the pastoral narrative
works of the Renaissance, these relationships and contextua-
lizations are achieved by seeking common vehicles of expression, a language that the followers of the genre identify as
their own. This renders the works coherent, with a *vraisemblance* of their own derived from their common ground of
intelligibility.

But just as this practice of repetition, "quotation" of
words, names, lines and metric forms brings to these works a

---

(20) Jonathan Culler refers to the importance of this relation of texts
to a body of maxims or rules as a mode of *vraisemblance* that involves
". . . a specifically literary intelligibility: a set of literary norms to
which texts may be related and by virtue of which they become meaningful and coherent" in *Structuralist Poetics, op. cit.*, p. 145.

(21) Erich Auerbach provides a brief discussion of this aspect in
*Literary Language and its Public in Late Latin Antiquity and the Mid-
dle Ages*, Princeton, The Bollingen Series, Princeton University Press,
1965, p. 262. Auerbach refers specifically to common experiences
which are shaped and recalled by the repetition of liturgical chants.

special sort of instant recognition, an identification with shared aesthetic experiences, the same repetitions may bring to the field of art different, even opposite consequences. The fixation that results from the repetition of formulas, from making *découpages* out of characters, names, situations, and events, when carried to an extreme can lead to a petrification, to an attempt to actually halt the process of interpretation. This is an aspect of pastoral to which contemporary readers react strongly and it must be dealt with in detail here. In the efforts to provide fixed formulas which can be recalled and names to identify without an intermediary elaboration, the pastoral convention of giving identical proper names (e.g. Amarillys, Galatea) and using category names (the oaten flute, Arcadia) for pastoral instruments and physical locations seems to be an attempt to deprive the situations, the characters, and the language that they use of any kind of ambiguity.

Since Plato (*Symposium, Cratylus*) this, and similar problems related to the use of language, particularly the difficulties in naming things to capture a constantly changing universe, have been one of the main concerns of language and of literary art. In the *Cratylus*, Socrates asks:

> Is it then possible to predicate of it rightly, if it is even vanishing, first that it is 'that' and next that it is of such or such a nature, or must it not ever, while the words are in our mouths, straightway become other, and slip away and no longer be the same. (22)

In fixing characters and situations by "quoting," that is, by repeating identical proper names and characteristics of physical "loci" from work to work, pastoral works present an intriguing answer to the Socratic question. At the same time,

---

(22) *The Dialogues of Plato*, from the translation of Benjamin Jowett, New York, Horace Liveright, 1930, p. 175.

their answer is a refusal to admit, to surrender to the necessary flow of time and to risk new interpretations.

Proper Names as Archetypes

Since Theocritus' *Idylls* (23) a number of particular names have been used to represent the identity of the characters of pastoral works; names such as Daphnis, Idylls I, V-VII, IX, XXVII; Tyrsis (to goad), Idyll I; Galatea (the fair one) Idyll V, XI, Corydon (the lark), Idyll IV; Tityrus Idyll III; Amarillys (golden), Idyll III, VI; and even Melampus (24) a dog in Idyll III. There are also names from mythology, in addition to Venus and Zeus, there is Pan, Idyll I; Cypris, Idyll I, II, XX; Ariadne, Idyll II; and Circe, Idyll II among others.

Virgil, the most famous renovator of pastoral poetry in imperial Rome, repeats the names used by Greek pastoral poets in his own *Eclogues* to name the shepherds as protagonists of his bucolic poems. The tremendous prestige of Virgil's works, both in his time and in the Renaissance, succeeded in establishing and continuing for a long period of time the convention of pastoral proper names. In his First Eclogue for instance, Tityrus reappears in his role as the calm shepherd, the guardian of sheep and Amarillys as the shepherdess object of the narrator's love. In the Eighth Eclogue, Tyrsis and Corydon are again the singing shepherds, victims, as their homonymous ancestors of unrequited love. Galatea, as the Galatea of countless poems and songs, is again the nympth, object of the attention and love of the singing shepherds. And in the Eclogues, there are the visits and interven-

---

(23) Theocritus, in turn, used names already found in Homer, in ancient mythology, and in earlier compositions of the Syracusan School of poetry. The names of Galatea and Daphnis are two examples.

(24) "Melampus," 'black spotted'. Also the name of a medicine man and prophet who cured women from madness. Cf. Sir William Smith, *Smaller Classical Dictionary*, New York, Dutton, 1958, pp. 186, 238.

tions of the familiar mythological gods, particularly Venus and Pan.

The repetition and even reappearance of the same character with the same name becomes, in some cases, archetypical. Galatea, Polyphemus, Silenus, Tityrus, Daphnis, Nysa, and even the dogs, along with others, become archetypical in the sense that they are synthesizers, embodiments of precise and identifiable feelings. Unlike allegories, they are not standing for or replacing a concept or an idea; instead they, their characters, are the epitomes of the given passion or sentiment they have suffered or have provoked.

In Renaissance pastoral poetry and especially in the narratives that flourished in the European literatures more closely influenced by the Greco-Roman cultures, the repetition of these pastoral characters, their proper names, and the expressions and songs were not only maintained but became the object of parodic distortions and critiques (25) and only after the genre's popularity had declined did the practice finally disappear. There are Galateas in Montemayor's *Los siete libros de la Diana* and Galatea is indeed both the title and main character of Cervantes' first pastoral (1585). When Honoré d'Urfé writes his pastoral novel *L'Astrée*, the nymph Galatea is again a protagonist in the multi-leveled plot of unsynchronized love.

With the same frequency as the main character of Galatea and Polyphemus the names and characters of Tyrsis and Corydon reappear and indeed are reincarnated in the majority of pastoral stories (e.g. *La Galatea*, Books I, II). These two have even been recently recreated—albeit with different intentions—by André Gide—Tityrus in *Paludes* and Corydon in a novel of the same name. And there are Nisidas and

---

(25) The French author Charles Sorel in his novel *Le Berger Extravagant* (1628) is the most obvious case, but Cervantes himself, not long after writing his own pastoral, *La Galatea* (1585) parodied and criticized the genre. He did it in *El coloquio de los perros* (1613) and in *Don Quijote* (1605) as well.

Amarillys, both in *La Galatea* (Libro Segundo) and in *L'Astrée* (3ème Partie), as well as new and poeticized names sounding as close to the "conventional" names as possible. The repetition of poeticized or pastorailized names is not confined to the characters alone. Because the intention of these identifications seems to be to include all elements of the physical, the natural world, the pastoral even apply the repetition of names and characters to the sphere of animals. This is seen in the peculiar insistence on repeating the names and characteristics of the shepherds' dogs.

"Melampo" and "Adro," for instance, in *Arcadia's* Prosa 2, were animals that had played a literary and practical role in earlier works. Melampo had helped the shepherds in Theocritus' Idyll III and Adro perhaps appeared as the faithful companion of Ulysses (26), or possibly as a hound. Melampo, already in Sanazzaro's work the archetype of the pastoral dog reappears not only in Cervantes' *La Galatea* (27) but in many other pastorals including several episodes of *L'Astrée*. In the Première Partie "Melamp" is again the epitome of the guardian of sheep. In la Deuxième Partie, however, the dog is part of an emblem in a painting the shepherds describe:

Vous avez raison, Dit Diane, même que je vois ici Melampe couché à ses pieds. Il est bien reconnaissable aux marques qu'il porte. Voyez la moitié de la tête, comme il l'a blanche. . . . On n'y a pas même oublié cette bande noire et blanche tout le long des jambes. Silvandre s'approchant d'elle: Et moi, dit-il, j'y reconnais entre ce troupeu la brebis qu'Astrée aime le plus. (28)

---

(26) "Adro" is perhaps a derivation of the Latin "latro" (a barker) or in another sense, a thief or animal of prey. It could also be a modified version of the name "Argos," the faithful dog of Ulysses, who died after seeing his master back from his journeys (Homer, *The Odyssey*, XVII).

(27) *La Galatea*, Libro Primero. The Spanish "Manchado" is a version of the Greek Melampus.

(28) Honoré d'Urfé, *L'Astrée*, Genette edition, *op. cit.*, pp. 125-126.

In this passage, the name of the dog, his markings, his colors are the same as in La Première Partie, but now, by virtue of the perfection with which he played his role, "Melamp" has been incorporated into the "picture" of perfect pastoral time and has become an emblem of himself. The same happens with the sheep.

This is important for two reasons. Not only does d'Urfé's passage illustrate the durability of the convention involved in the repetition of names, but this convention itself illustrates how the elements of the natural surroundings represent the theme of the world of order and reliability in contrast to the theme of the human passions, so fully developed in the pastoral.

This total identification of characters, surroundings, and ways of living (supposedly shepherding) with other identical characters and situations of earlier times poses interesting questions which the authors of pastorals themselves faced. How is it possible to have a unique identity when the persons —even if they are characters of fiction—are also totally identical to someone else? This question about names and identities, alive since classical times (e.g. in Aristotle's *De Anima* and in the works of the Stoics), gained a renewed and intense interest in the Renaissance and was dealt with in a variety of ways. One result of that interest were the treatises of the Spanish grammarians Juan and Alfonso de Valdés and of other humanists such as Huarte de San Juan, Francisco de Medina, Ambrosio de Morales, and the poets Fernando de Herrera and Fray Luis de León, to name only a few.

This homogenization of names was not the only way given by pastoral authors to solve these problems. Cervantes, following this pastoral convention even in his first pastoral, instead of shifting to pastoral names, used several versions of a particular one, thus pastoralizing it even more. In the Libro Tercero of *La Galatea*, for instance, we find two close versions of the name Orfenio/Orfino, and in Libro Primero, Marsilo/Marsilio, and finally a less close one, Artidoro/

Arsildo (29). These slight modifications probably provoked a renewed interest in the character and perhaps a touch of humor. For the more erudite readers, this might set off the search for the closer precedent in other pastoral works such as the Virgilian *Eclogues* or Sanazzaro's *Arcadia.* What is undeniable is that this apparent confusion calls the attention of the audience to the material at hand and reminds it once more of the convention itself.

Another version of this convention is the case of the poet who disguises his name, adopting in its place a pastoral-sounding one. Such is the case of Sanazzaro appearing in *Arcadia* as Sincero, Virgil who intervenes in the Fifth Eclogue under the name of Menalcas, and the case of Sir Philip Sidney disguising his participation in his *Arcadia* under the name of Pyrocles (30).

Yet another aspect, related to this, is the disguising of historical figures under the names and characteristics of pastoral figures. This is not exclusive to the pastoral genre but is common in pastorals which from their publication were intended as what is known now as *romans-à-clef.* Typical examples are Gálvez de Montalvo's *El Pastor de Fílida* (1582) entire sections of *La Galatea* (1585), and many sections of *L'Astrée* (1630) and countless lesser pastorals (31).

---

(29) These changes or variations in names which, for a long time, were considered as uncertainties in Cervantes' artistry, have been brilliantly analyzed by Leo Spitzer. He studies the multiplicity of perspectives provided by Cervantes through the use of polynomasia for his characters. Cf. Spitzer's paper "On the Significance of Don Quijote" published posthumously in *MLN*, Vol. 77, Number 2, March 1962: 113-129 and also "Linguistic Perspectivism in the Don Quijote," in *Linguistics and Literary History*, Princeton, Princeton University Press, 1974.

(30) Cf. Miguel de Cervantes, *La Galatea*, Chas Fitzmaurice-Kelly, ed., H. Oelsner and A. B. Welford, translators, Glasgow, Gowans and Gray, 1903, editor's introduction, p. xxxi.

(31) Materials to support this can be found in the collection of quotations assembled by Fleming Green Vinson, *A Critical Bibliography of the Spanish Pastoral Novel, 1559-1633*, unpublished Ph.D. dissertation, University of North Carolina at Chapel Hill, 1969, already quoted.

Category Nouns

The search for literary devices that would facilitate a shared artistic language does not end with the repetition of proper names given to the characters and even to the animals. Another device is found in the use of category nouns (32).

When Sanazzaro, many centuries after the Virgilian reintroduction of the pastoral eclogue, composed his *Arcadia* (1504), he recovered not only the names of the characters but also their exact modes of expression. To this he added a number of other features from the Italian poetic traditions including the use of meters of versification—terza rima, ottava rima, etc. to be discussed below.

Interestingly Sanazzaro repeated the names of the physical "natural" elements, the flora and rivers. Landscapes are re-enacted and recognizable to an erudite audience in his version of the "arcadian" world. These are recognizable—not because he emphasized the "natural" world but because he copied the names and qualities that Virgil used in his *Eclogues*, particularly in Eclogue VII.

The first chapter—Prosa Prima—of Sanazzaro's *Arcadia*, was most influential among the pastorals of the Renaissance. It is devoted almost entirely to a classification by enumeration of each of the trees and hedges that are part of the location of the story along with the classical connotations. Only at the end of the description do two characters, under the "pastoralized" poetic names of Ergasto and Selvagio, make their appearance on the scene:

---

(32) Linguists, philosophers, and social scientists have long been interested in the subject. Claude Lèvi-Strauss in *The Savage Mind"* discusses precisely how proper names can become common nouns and vice versa. Lèvi-Strauss concludes that there is no fundamental difference between the two, but rather that proper names lie upon the margin of classificatory systems, marking their limits, but ready to augment or diminish their semantic load," p. 85.

*Quivi senza nodo veruno si vede il drittissimo abete, nato
a sostenere i pericolo del mare; e con più aperti rami la
robusta quercia, e l'alto frassino, e lo amenissimo platano
vi si distendono.* (33)

In addition to the adjectives employed to stress the beauty
of the delightful clearing at the summit of the *non umile*
wood, each of the species of trees, as individual examples or
as groups representing the family are identified by the most
representative feature associated with the species.

We find in careful enumeration the *drittissimo* abete, the
robusta quercia, the *alto* frassino, *amenissimo* platano,
noderoso castagno, *fronzuto* bosco, and *eccelso* pino, followed by the *ombroso* faggio, *incorruptibile* tiglia, *fragile*
tamarisco, and *orientale* palma. This careful and detailed ex-
position gives the audience a sense, by way of adjectival epi-
thets, of the perfection as well as the delightful character of
the place. The enumeration of the floral species in this and
other pastoral works and the profusion of adjectives employed here have been considered of fundamental significance since they are instrumental in describing the pleasantness of the location—the *locus amoenus*—and as such, this is
a pastoral convention.

From other points of view this classificatory concern has
also been viewed as an attempt to create a sense of reality
since the botannical items enumerated are plausible empirical
specimens that one could find in the actual mountains where
the action has been set. But these classifications and enumer-
ations, as given in the above example, serve, in my view, another function of greater importance in the total panorama
of the aesthetics of these works. Looking at the paragraphs of
Arcadia one can observe that the characteristics attributed to
the real, actual trees and hedges are not totally arbitrary,

---

(33) Jacopo Sanazzaro, *Arcadia*, Luigi Portirelli, ed., Milano, Societá
Tipografica de' Classici Italiani, 1806, pp. 1-2.

even in their function as hyperbolic descriptions of the beauty of the trees. Oaks are sturdy, ashes lofty, chestnuts knotty, and beeches provide a most refreshing shade. The respective leafiness of the box tree, the durability of the linden, the fragility of the tamarisk, and the oriental origins of the palm are also strong associations fixed by use and custom in coined phrases, clichés that at once explain and elude explanation. The trees enumerated in Sanazzaro's text are not individual specimens,particular trees that happen to be and could possibly be at the pleasant summit of the actual Mount Parthenio; they, in their categorical form, are the symbol/model of the species. As such they are real and unreal at the same time. The Arcadian trees are real because one could find trees that show these attributes but they are unreal because they are not individual trees but essences.

In these categorizations or objectivations by repeated, euphemized proper names, by category nouns, or by hyperboles that provide an extra-descriptive value, there is what W. W. Holdheim has defined as a "pervasive stylistic intention" (34). The clichés created about the Lignon River, the dog Melampus, or the poet Daphnis succeed in accomplishing seemingly contradictory results. On the one hand, they provide a sense of coherent, uncomplicated reality. There is *the* river, *the* animals, *the* poet.

But, of course, rivers, animals, and people do not exist in this form. This shear availability, as Holdheim argues in his discussion of the function of the cliché, reveals a pre-arranged interpretation. That seemingly uncomplicated immediacy ". . . corresponds to a reality which has been artificially rendered so unproblematical that there seems to be nothing to interpret, and is a highly stylized thing" (35).

---

(34) W. W. Holdheim, "Description and Cliché," *Arcadia* 70 (1978): 1-9.
(35) *Ibid.*, p. 3.

And this is precisely the intent of the artistic manipulation of pastoral. In those contrived paradises described above, nothing related to the physical surroundings is intended as factual, "real." Those idyllic *loci* correspond to a view of nature that is eternal, immutable, and therefore free from human interpretation, though this itself implies a definite interpretation. What these works present as unclear, complex, amiss is the variety and confusion of human passions.

The clichés described above succeed in exploiting the expressive possibilities of language in ways that would seem paradoxical at first glance. First, they attempt to solve the ambiguity of language and the changeability of meanings in names, words, nouns by connecting the given qualities—beauty in the river, fidelity in the dog, art in the poet—to the essences of each of the specific examples. At the same time, and by virtue of the identification resulting from this, the clichés facilitate a communication among those cultivated élite audiences who share the knowledge and understanding that those linguistic devices imply or express. The artistic manipulation of language involved in this process of identification and stylization is carried in the Renaissance pastorals to all aspects of expression.

Quotations and "Literary Découpages"

Just as the elements of nature and the characters have a fixed name and an identical role, the characters of these narratives express their thoughts in identical manner, frequently using identical words. I have already mentioned the effective way in which Sanazzaro, in composing his *Arcadia*, recovered modes of expression not only from classical pastorals but also from authors who were masters of the Italian tongue. Sanazzaro using earlier pastorals (particularly from Theocritus and Virgil), re-elaborated the situations, sentimental problems, and the characters' language in the closest possible translations. From Boccaccio, Petrarch, and others, he took the style and innovations they introduced in the metric art.

As an example of the first, we find a recounted history of the pastoral genre in Prosa Decima of *Arcadia*, told as if it were in the words of the authors themselves. This history is retold from an initiation by the god Pan through the composition of the "shepherd of Syracuse" (36) to the works of the "Mantuan Tityrus."

In this reincarnation, the pastoral poet repeats literally a number of expressions already known as clichés in the literary circles of the Italian school. The narrator says:

> *Per la qual cosa Titiro lieto di tanto onore, con questa medesima sampogna dilettandosi, insegnò primieramente la selve di risonare il nome della formosa Amarillida (37); Ma avende costui dalla natura lo ingegno a più alte cose disposto, e non contentandosi di sì umile suono, vi cangiò quella canna che voi ora vi vedete più grossa, e più che le altre nova, per poter meglio cantare le cose maggiore, e fare le selve degne degli altissimi Consoli (38) di Roma. (39)*

The repetitions of classical expressions found in these lines are so obvious that they are likely to be dismissed as clear illustrations of conventional imitation. And Sanazzaro is not an isolated case.

---

(36) After Virgil's Eclogue III, "Prima syracosio dignata est ludere versu."

(37) After Virgil's Eclogue I, 1-5, "formosam resonare doces Amaryllida silvas."

(38) Here again, as in the Greek poems, the intentionality of the authors of pastoral in creating a more effective kind of poetic language is repeated.

(39) Jacopo Sanazzaro, *Arcadia*, Luigi Portirelli, ed., p. 135.

Just as the authors of pastoral used proper names, words, and whole sentences from works of classical times, the authors of Renaissance pastorals lifted complete sentences, passages, and portions of poems from authors in their own vernacular languages (e.g. Petrarch) and from recognized masters of earlier times. This practice has been studied under the rubric of imitation and/or influence. Yet it is, according to the internal *vraisamblance* rules of this genre, part of the aesthetics of identification and cultivation of an artistic language, an intentional effort.

An example notable for its popularity and durability, particularly in the pastorals of the Iberian peninsula, is the repeated use of the verses dedicated to the beloved *esquiva*. In a famous dialogue of *La Galatea* the shepherd Damon sings:

¡Oh más que el cielo, oh más que el sol hermosa,
y para mí más dura que un diamante,
presta a mi mal, y al bien muy perezosa
¿Cuál abrego, cuál cierzo, cual levante
te sopló de aspereza, que así ordenas
que huiga el paso, y no te esté delante? (40)

As many scholars and critics of Cervantine art have pointed out these lines and the structure of the exclamatory epithet reproduce similar structures and lines used by other Renaissance authors, concretely by the early Renaissance Spanish master Garcilaso de la Vega.

A most successful poet and admirer of Italianate poetry, Garcilaso, in his Egloga I addresses his beloved, comparing hyperbolically the hard cold response of Galatea to the hardness of marble and to the coldness of snow:

---

(40) Miguel de Cervantes, *La Galatea*, Avalle-Arce, editor, p. 109.

¡Oh más dura que mármol a mis quejas,
y al encendido fuego en que me quemo
más helada que nieve, Galatea. (Égloga I, 57-59) (41)

The prestige of Garcilaso alone cannot account for Cervantes' repetition of his lines. In Cervantes' case and in that of others, the appropriation of lines is not an indication of a lack of inspiration or skill. The recurrent use and elaboration of earlier and very well known works is a sign, a testimony to an intentional poetic mastery which the pastoral authors cultivated and sought. The more obvious and well integrated those *découpages* were, the better the proof of the authors' knowledge and skill.

The fact of recurrence of forms and themes has been well documented. Francisco López Estrada, for instance, in his study of Cervantes' *La Galatea* (42), traces the numerous links of the book to major authors of the Italian Renaissance. But merits emphasis that it is neither accidental nor merely an exercise in imitation that the best authors of pastoral incorporated complete lines and sentences taken from other authors of the past. They incorporated those works as part of the *vraisemblance* of the pastoral genre, as a convention or trademark which, when successfully managed, indicated their artistic mastery.

Thus the following lines of Montemayor's *Diana* can be and undoubtedly were read as an intended identification with such prestigious authors as Virgil, Theocritus, Petrarch, as well as with other masters of the Italian and Spanish languages:

---

(41) Garcilaso de la Vega, *Obras*, Madrid, Clásicos castellanos, Espasa-Calpe, 1961, p. 26.
(42) Francisco López Estrada, *op. cit.*, pp. 51-117.

Sylvano:
Pastora mía, más blanca y colorada
que ambas rosas por abril cogidas,
y más resplandeciente (43)

Several consequences merit closer scrutiny. First, followers of the pastoral genre would recognize the characteristics expected in a protagonist of pastoral themes in the hyperbolic description of the shepherdess. Second, they would also expect the authors to describe the heroes or heroines of those stories in extremely laudatory or encomiastic terms. And finally, better educated audiences would link those protagonists' characteristics with the characteristics attributed to the repeated Galateas of the past. They would identify the passages where they were described and would appreciate the artistry involved in the composition. All audiences, élite and common alike, would identify and appreciate the fact that their chosen author would not only repeat the words and expressions of the famous authors but they also had mastered the complicated forms of versification and rhymes cultivated in the genre.

Metric Forms of Versification

Although pastorals did not exclusively use any particular metric form, certain ones were definitely favored. Occasionally forms were used simply to transpose as faithfully as possible the works of some masters of the author's own vernacular language. That was the case in many of the Spanish and French pastorals. Other meters were chosen because of the

---

(43) Jorge de Montemayor, *Los siete libros de la Diana*, Francisco López Estrada, ed., Madrid, Clásicos castellanos, Espasa-Calpe, 1967, p. 277.

success of the Italian innovators of the Renaissance. Forms such as the terza rima, ottava rima, sextine, sonnet, and madrigal were to be frequently used.

Since Boccaccio's *Il Ninfale Fiesolano* (1477) one of the metric forms favored in later pastorals of the Renaissance was the ottava rima: stanzas of eight hendecasyllabic lines rhyming in alternating lines and ending with a couplet—ABABABCC. This form (also favored in chivalric epics by Pulci, Boiardo, and Ariosto) became, after Boccaccio's pastoral tale, one of the conventional rhymes. Ottavas are the most frequent forms of versification in *Arcadia* and most of the Italian pastorals; and Cervantes' *Galatea* begins precisely with four *octavas reales*, the Spanish adaptation of the Italian form (44).

Mientras que al triste lamentable acento
del mal acorde son del canto mïo,
en Eco amarga de cansado aliento
responde el monte, el prado, el llano, el rïo
. . . . (45)

In spite of the success of the ottava rima, as demonstrated in the numerous adaptations of that form throughout the Southern European literatures, some critics maintain that this composition was considered less refined a form than the terza rima, which according to Greg (46), became the standard form of Renaissance pastoral. Greg in this case is apparently

---

(44) The use of the ottava rima did not end with the pastorals of the Renaissance. It was very popular in baroque lyric poetry (e.g. in Góngora). Later, in the Romantic period, poets such as Byron, Keats, and Espronceda, among others, reintroduced this long and dignified meter. They introduced also the themes of melancholy and quasi-heroic deeds of individuals that are related by these discursive poems in pastoral.

(45) Miguel de Cervantes, *op. cit., loc. cit.*, see note.

(46) W. W. Greg, *op. cit.*, p. 31.

speaking exclusively of the verse and dramatic eclogues that proliferated in the Neo-Latin literatures of the Renaissance, but the terza rima stanza was indeed used for all kinds of versions of pastoral and, as such, was adopted internationally. This metric form, also appropriated for pastoral compositions after Boccaccio (47), consists of a three-line stanza usually in iambic pentameter in which the second line of each trio rhymes with the first and third lines of the following trio of verses: ABA, BCB, CDC, etc. The long and balanced lines modulated by the cesura and the recurrent equilibrium of the rhyme made this type of stanza a favorite for expressing a wide range of emotions. Sanazzaro, in this Ecloga Undecima, used the terza rima to depict his sad, wretched situation at the death of his mother. On other occasions (Ecloga II, III, IX, X) he used it to praise the mountains, the day of the nymphs' birthdays, or the merits of the shepherds' songs.

After Sanazzaro's *Arcadia*, we find the terza rima in compositions praising nature, in elegies, and most frequently in pastoral complaints.

With the metric forms, the copying of other authors reveals the interest in adaptation, renewal of the poet's own literature. Because of the difficulties inherent in the techniques of versification and the peculiar characteristics of each national language, the skill of the poet underwent a definite test. The best authors succeeded in blending all technical and linguistic aspects of their own language to the demands of the different meters and rhymes while also maintaining the elaborate sentimental themes which the pastoral genre and its audiences demanded.

By the end of the sixteenth century and the beginning of the seventeenth, the taste and sophistication of the literary

---

(47) The perfecting of this metric form is attributed to Boccaccio. He first used terza rima in an eclogue of his *Ameto*. Cf. Greg, *op. cit.*, p. 31.

elites demanded an ever-increasing complication of language, metric forms, and other literary conceits. This is perhaps why, in the pastorals of the Iberian peninsula and those from the French Renaissance, it is not possible to affirm that any particular form of metric versification was favored over any other one. The convention was to demonstrate the greatest skills in all possible kinds of compositions, a fashion that continued for a long time thereafter. This is, at any rate, the effect I deduce from reading the pastorals published after *La Diana*.

Among the most complicated, and also best adapted, metric forms found in the pastorals of the late sixteenth and early seventeenth centuries were sextines (48), liras (49) and its derivations, canción (50), and madrigals (51). These derivations, particularly popular in Spain, were also cultivated very successfully by the poets of France.

Examples of the metric compositions favored by authors of pastoral, illustrate that the conventionalized forms of versification served as vehicles of adaptation of new means of

------

(48) Sextine: a six-line stanza which, like the sonnet, was perfected by Petrarch and was used throughout Europe during the Renaissance. A beautiful sextine appears in *La Galatea*, Primero Libro, "En áspera, cerrada, escura noche . . . ," *op. cit.*, p. 77. An analysis of a *sestina* from *La Diana* is given in Chapter V.

(49) Lira: a five-line stanza of alternating heptasyllabic and endecasyllabic verses in the form aBabB.

(50) Derived from the Italian *canzone*, it alternates heptasyllabic and endecasyllabic lines and was also popularized by Petrarch. Garcilaso wrote several that became classical examples in Spanish literature: "Con un manso ruido/de agua corriente y clara . . ." rates among the best.

(51) The madrigal is again a combination of heptasyllabic and endecasyllabic verses. It is usually short and involves a complicated line of thought. Its themes are usually love or contemplation of nature. The classic Spanish madrigal "Ojos claros, serenos . . ." has the following pattern: aBBcDdCcaA. The pattern of combined lines is variable, however.

expression as well as ways of identifying with their own national masters and with the masters of the genre regardless of their nationality.

Pastorals, in fact, exploited to the maximum all forms of italianate versification (52). Their success, of course, lies in the integration of those forms with the other well-established, familiar forms of versification. In the pastorals of France and Spain we find frequent instances of national ballads, villancicos, coplas, as well as themes from medieval pastourelles side by side with classical Greco-roman figures and others expressing their complaints in Petrarchan forms. An example of this combination will be provided in Chapter VI.

We can conclude from these examples that the cultivation of a particular form of art requires the use of and emphasis on specific rules: carefully considered kinds of language, arguments, and forms of expression. Manifest in these repetitions and incorporations of other works is an awareness on the author's part of the effect that well-known expressions can have in poetic language. Since the beginning of poetry, the repetition of words and sounds has been of basic importance (53). However, what the authors of these highly contrived and "conventional" pastorals demonstrate is the ironic power and effect that which is well-known and supposedly weak can have for literary art.

---

(52) See the *Pastorella* in Mia Gerhardt, *Essai d'analyse littéraire de la Pastorale dans les littératures italienne, espagnole et française*. The Hague, Van Gorcum, 1950, pp. 38-39, and the prologue to Montemayor's *La Diana, op. cit.*, p. lvi.

(53) It is interesting to note that around the time of the acme of pastoral's popularity, a number of songbooks and collections of most of the genuine Spanish folk ballads were published. Important examples were the *Cancionero de Romances* (Antwerp, 1550), *Silva de varios Romances* (Zaragoza, 1550), as well as other miscellany of ballads and romances.

The questions that the major authors of pastoral confronted and solved were the continual manipulation of an artistic language in such a way that the ordinary, well-known, established, and even the commonplace could gain enlarged significance, precisely because the terms were already in the common domain.

CHAPTER IV

LANGUAGE: RHETORICAL CONVENTIONS

Seen against the background of the Renaissance view of art, artistic language is a powerful instrument for the acquisition of knowledge and the expression of human concerns. The word can expose, compare, enhance, and correct, but it can also hide and deceive. When these characteristics of language become the instrument of art, the artistic word becomes the best vehicle to express, illustrate, or exercise those thoughts and feelings that a more direct, obvious discourse would render ordinary and trite. Awareness of the difficulties in expressing complicated feelings and thoughts via language as a medium is the basis of rhetoric and it is a major concern in pastoral aesthetics.

This is not to say that pastoral is the only genre that took up the matters of artistic verbal expression nor that the contrast between the contrived and the real as central to its task is exclusive to this genre. Pastoral, however, adheres to a number of rules or principles of coherence—what, as discussed in Chapter II, was known in the sixteenth century as *decorum* (1), and in contemporary criticism as *vraisemblance*

---

(1) *Decorum*: Ursula Kuhm, in her study of literary terms, lists this term as it was defined by the theoreticians in England. Puttenham, for instance, following Aristotelian principles in his *Arte of English Poesie*,

(2). These rules reflect, in the individual works and in the genre as a whole, self-referentiality.

There is in pastoral an intentional, systematic contrivance at the linguistic as well as the rhetorical levels of composition, which in close interaction with the thematic, philosophical and theoretical levels constitute the center of action and development in pastoral works. In pastoral aesthetics, there is a studied coherence between the philosophical and theoretical principles (the macro-contexts) and the linguistic and rhetorical elements (the micro-contexts) that act as vehicles of expression within those general currents, general principles.

In the previous chapter, I examined the characteristic pastoral re-appropriations of category nouns, cliché-like sentences and pastoral proper names as an attempt to develop a kind of identification with characters, authors, and texts of earlier pastorals. This form of artistic recuperation, typical of the genre, is strengthened in the pastorals of the Renaissance by the use of specific rhetorical devices. These figures, tropes and forms of poetic license, although not exclusive to pastorals, complement the search for more refined expression, a more effective tool of communication so important for the poetics of the genre. In the previous chapter I analyzed only some examples of the most characteristic names, category

---

defined *decorum* as decency, seemliness, *analogia*. Ursula Kuhm, *English Literary terms in Poetological Texts in the Sixteenth Century*, Salzburg, unpublished Ph.D. dissertation, University of Münster, 1974, p. 161.

(2) Jonathan Culler distinguishes several levels of "vraisemblablisation": 1) within the works of a genre, 2) within a particular individual work among the elements, 3) between the theme chosen and the expression (it is possible to relate this particular sort of "vraisemblance" to the concept of *decorum* in Renaissance aesthetics), 4) between the audience's expectations and the work as a vehicle for expressing experiences in a language other than the ordinary. *Structuralist Poetics,* Ithaca, *op. cit.*, especially pp. 137 and ff.

nouns and expression-cliché, in this chapter I will describe only some of the most prominent rhetorical figures and tropes as they relate both to the stylization of the language, and to the thematic purpose of the books. Of course, the language, rhetorical figures and themes together form the coherent whole of the work and it is only for analytical purposes that I have classified their functions separately in this study.

In this chapter I will concentrate on the relationship between the cultivation of literary rhetorical devices and art as an epistemological tool in four of the major Renaissance pastoral narratives: Sanazzaro's *Arcadia*, Montemayor's *Los siete libros de la Diana*, Cervantes' *La Galatea*, and d'Urfé's *L'Astrée*.

Emphasis throughout will be on the very particular pastoral arrangement of literary language, in which words, forms, and rhetorical principles are manipulated and purposefully stylized. The conventional contrivances employed in these stylizations are clearly related to the abovementioned awareness of the powers of artistic language. In the cases that I have chosen, they rest specifically on the possibility of expressing the most complicated concepts and feelings with syntactic and rhetorical means.

The first part of the chapter deals with the emphasis on and intensification of language through the uses of hyperbole, reiteration, and hyperbaton. The second part will deal with the manipulation of poetic language under the disguise of apparently effortless and simple expressions, i.e. the supposed language of the shepherds. In analyzing the specific words, the poetic irony (3) involved in this latter form of

---

(3) I use here the trope irony in the sense Northrop Frye defines it in his description of the ironic mode: "The term irony, then, indicates a technique of appearing to be less than one is. . . . The ironic fiction-writer, then, deprecates himself and, like Socrates, pretends to know nothing, even that he is ironic." *Anatomy of criticism: Four Essays*, Princeton, Princeton University Press, 1973, p. 40.

artistic creativity, will be emphasized suggesting that this is perhaps one of the most important aspects or features of pastoral aesthetics. This irony (which was probably more clearly perceived when pastoral works flourished and were in vogue) has been one of the reasons that pastoral narratives have been so difficult for modern audiences to grasp.

The intensifying/simplifying use of language and certain rhetorical devices will be stressed over many other equally important and widespread pastoral devices for three reasons. First, by putting the most complex matters in a refined but simplified way and by emphasizing rhetorical devices, pastoral literature illustrates the ability of art to create illusory realities which so differ from the empirical nature of other human activities. Second, the combination of simple, "pure" literary art, on the one hand, and complex modes of expression on the other, is a recurrent mode of stylization in the literature of Western cultures (4). Finally, this double aspect of the use of artistic language is particularly important because the use of controlled language permits specific coherence among the thematic, formal, and linguistic elements of the genre. In particular, it makes explicit the interplay between sophistication and complexity of human existence and the simplicity of the natural background.

Although it is also possible to trace and analyze the characteristic modes of stylization of the pastoral narratives from the thematic point of view, a formal perspective provides the clearest view of the interplay between the elements and stylization. The thematic and structural conventional characteristics of pastoral aesthetics will be analyzed in Chapter V.

---

(4) Both views have a long, prestigious history. Simplicity and purity of expression was advocated by Cicero, Quintilian, and others in Classical Rome, again later in Neoclassic aesthetics, and in modern times by Symbolist poets, among others. Stress on the complexity of forms similarly has a long tradition; e.g. in Baroque aesthetics.

Artistic mediation makes it possible to differentiate between empirical facts and artistic, fictional facts. While authors as artists can describe natural scenes (empirical worlds), and we the audience can relate to them, there are also other experiences and realities that are much more difficult to describe in ordinary terms. Here the role of artistic expression, contrivances that are at the center of pastoral poetics (one of the micro-contexts), come into clear focus.

Whether explicitly discussed or approached through ironic hints that underscore concern with the artistic activity, this issue comes repeatedly to the fore in the pastoral romances chosen for my analysis. In *La Galatea* for instance, the need to provide a new vehicle of expression, a "tercera naturaleza" as Cervantes calls it in Book Six, is perhaps the most important leit-motif. At times, this new, third level of expression appears as the confluence of the sounds of learned art (musical instruments) and the sounds of nature (songs of birds):

> *Y era de suerte que, concordándose of son de la triste música y el de la alegre armonía de los jilguerillos, calandrias y ruiseñores, y el amargo de los profundos gemidos, formaba todo junto un tan extraño concento* [sic] *, que no hay lenguna que encarecerlo pueda.* (5)

In other instances, the difference between the artistic and ordinary description is conveyed via similes and comparison:

> *No poca maravilla me causa, Elicio, la incomparable belleza destas frescas riberas, y no sin razón, porque quien ha visto como yo, las espaciosas del nombrado Betis, y las*

---

(5) Miguel de Cervantes, *La Galatea*, edited by Juan Bautista Avalle-Arce, Madrid, Clásicos castellanos, 1961, Libro Sexto, p. 176.

*que visten y adornan al famoso Ebro y al conocido Pisuerga
. . . sin dejar de haber rodeado las frescuras del apacible
Sebeto, grande ocasión había de ser la que a maravilla me
moviese de ver otras algunas. . . . Sin duda puedes creer
que la amenidad y frescura de las riberas deste río hace
notoria y conocida ventaja a todas las que has nombrado.*
(6)

There are yet other cases in which the search for a new,
"third" level of communication is expressed by stressing the
difficulties of describing accurately the attributes of places or
the beauty of the shepherdesses who are the object of the
poet/shepherds love. This is, for instance, the case of Galatea
whose description lies beyond the scope of normal words:

*Galatea, cuya hermosura era tanta que sería mejor dejarla
en su punto pues faltan palabras para encarcerla* (7)

And it is also the case of Astrée, whose beauty necessarily
(being as she is an epitome and paragon) exceeds the limits
of the descriptions conveyed in words.

*Il este vrai, dit-elle [Daphnide], qu'en cecy
la renommée est moindre que la verité, et qu'il
est certain que vostre **beauté surpasse ce que l'on en dit*** (8)

The difficulties of describing special subjects in ordinary
terms is constantly emphasized in these narratives, but the attention driven to the word itself and to artistic expressions
stresses their power and function even more. Since there are
no ordinary words that could adequately express the height-
ened feelings of sorrow in the first example and (the har-

---

(6) *Ibid.*, p. 169.
(7) *Ibid.*, Libro Primero, p. 54.
(8) Honoré d'Urfé, *L'Astrée*, Hugues Vaganay, ed., Lyon, P. Masson,
1925, IV, p. 330, emphasis mine.

mony of the *strange* concert) and the awe in the other two (the beauty of the ladies), the scene and the two women have to be described via special artifices. Pastoral rhetoric is the chosen vehicle. These reiterated assertions about the impossibility (9) of communicating something deeply felt are addressed through syntactic and stylistic arrangements whose aim it is to balance the form and the content of the works. When this balance fails, as it often did in some of the mediocre imitations (10) of the major works, the language loses the impact of its nuances and the expressions of the characters become mere rhetorical exercises.

Thus one of the features that marks the difference between masterpieces of this genre, and their secondary counterparts is precisely the balance those famous works of the genre display between the chosen expressions and the subjects to be discussed.

Given the nature of the feelings and passions so prominent as thematic concerns of these Renaissance pastorals, one of the most characteristic figures of pastoral language is hyperbole.

Hyperbole

As a figure of language, hyperbole is frequently employed for descriptive and character intensification. When, for ex-

___

(9) With respect to this question, and something that I have not seen discussed, the authors of the pastoral works that I am studying seem to be elaborating on the rhetorical figure *adynaton* or impossibilities. Michael C. J. Putnam gives a reference to the uses of adynaton as a rhetorical figure used by Virgil and quotes, as examples, verses 59-63 of the First Eclogue. Cf. *Virgil's Pastoral Art: Studies in the Eclogues*, Princeton, Princeton University Press, 1970, p. 51.

(10) For a good discussion about some secondary works in Spanish pastoral, cf. Juan Bautista Avalle-Arce, *La novela pastoril española*, Madrid, Istmo, 1974, especially Chapters IV and VI.

ample, Cervantes describes the heroines/shepherdesses or the feelings they inspire, he presents them in hyperbolic terms:

> *Su nombre era Nĭsida, y su hermosura tanta, que me atrevo a decir que la naturaleza cifró en ella el estremo de sus perfecciones, y . . . tan a una en ella la honestidad y la belleza, que lo que la una encendĭa la otra enfriaba, y los deseos que su gentileza hasta el más subido cielo levantaba, su honesta gravedad hasta lo más bajo de la tierra abatĭa.* (11)

As we saw before in the description of the landscape and rivers, the terms of the hyperbole in themselves direct attention to the need of the artistic language to deal with things or events that are out of the ordinary. But there are other purposes which make the hyperbole a favored rhetorical figure in pastoral romances. Given the multiple function of the role of these heroines in the total work, they have to be marked as different, as above the rest. In the particular case of the lady described here, her hyperbolic introduction is a way to identify her with the model of the story herself, with Galatea. This identification, which will be discussed in Chapter VI, is achieved among other things, by employing almost identical terms in describing the two characters. And this is one of the most significant functions of the hyperbole. But there are others which the aesthetics of pastoral exploits in the function of its aims.

Because the person and the feelings that person elicits are conveyed in the superlative, there is no other term of comparison, no possible referent but herself. Because she is beautiful in the extreme, and the feelings of awe she inspires are so elevated while earthly desire is brought down to its lowest point, these qualities become their own referent. Comparable

---

(11) *La Galatea*, Book II, p. 140, emphasis mine.

only to themselves, they exist within their own circular relationship: These ideal shepherdesses are clichés, so to speak, in themselves.

The process of intensification takes other forms. In *L'Astrée* for example, one speaker, Florice places "presque hors du monde" the beauty of the shepherdess and adds:

J'avoue, dit-elle, que j'ay esté aveugle de ne cognoistre pas que vous estiez la bergere Astrée, de qui la beauté, ne pouvant se renfermer en un si petit pays que le Forests, remplit de sa louange toutes les contrées d'alentour. (12)

Instead of using any special means of comparison—even the self-referential superlative—d'Urfé accomplishes the intensification through exaggeration: Astrée's beauty exceeds the constraints of a single place and its fame reaches beyond the limiting surroundings. This is a necessary intensificatory device since Astrée's role, as model, extends to other shepherdesses.

In other cases hyperbolic excess literally lifts the shepherds out of place, taking them to another realm:

El cual [Artidoro], sin hacerse de rogar, siguió su comenzado canto con tan extremada y maravillosa voz, que todos los que le escuchaban estaban transportados en oírla. (13)

Thus the importance of the shepherd's discourse is stressed by a variety of rhetorical means, and is effective as long as it keeps coherence between the means and the aims of the discourse (what is said and the way it is said).

---

(12) *L'Astrée*, H. Vaganay, ed., Book II, p. 121.
(13) *La Galatea*, Book II, p. 69.

Elsewhere similar intensificatory effects are achieved by the use of pleonasms (14), ellipses (15), hypotyposis—especially hyperbaton and anacoluthon—as well as other forms of syntactic and rhetorical figures i.e., synecdoches (see below) of all kinds of metaphors ("Galatea, nuevo milagro de hermosura" and metonymies ("Los pastores, no querrán consentir que se les quite delante de sus ojos *el sol* que los alumbra y *la discreción* que los admira, y *la belleza* que los incita y anima a mil honrosas competencias . . . Galatea") (16).

Francisco López Estrada, in his already cited *Estudio crítico* (1948), analyzes exhaustively the figures used by Cervantes in *La Galatea*. Jacques Ehrmann, in his *Un paradis désepéré: L'Amour et l'illusion dan l'Astrée* (1963), also discusses the uses and the purpose that the figures of artistic language have in *L'Astrée*. Most annotated editions of Sannazaro's *Arcadia*, such as Scherillo's edition and the earlier one by Corniani, include the uses of rhetorical figures in that work as well. Here I only point to the most frequently used throughout the pages of these major works, stressing those figures and tropes that best relate to the themes and to the structures later discussed in later chapters of this study.

---

(14) "Pleonasm" as well as its opposite "ellipse" were, according to Keniston already disappearing from Castilian literary use by the end of the sixteenth century, but were kept in many pastorals and in *Don Quijote* by Cervantes with parodic and stylistic purposes. Cf. Hayward Keniston, *The Syntax of Castilian Prose: The Sixteenth Century*, Chicago, The University of Chicago Press, 1937, p. 142.

(15) Hypotyposis consists in the fashioning of some grammatical change by altering the normal order of the syntax. This, which is frequent in oral communication, is also found in literary discourse. One type of hypotyposis is the anacoluthon which consists in the alteration of the normal syntactical order and is extremely frequent in colloquial speech. Literary examples of anacoluthon are numerous: "Antes rogó a los demas pastores que la escuchasen, pues, 'para lo poco que de mi cuento quedaba, tiempo habría de acabarlo." *La Galatea*, Avalle-Arce edition, Book II, p. 178.

(16) *La Galatea*, Libro Sexto, p. 167.

In addition to the intensificatory similes, hyperboles, and qualifiers on the limitations of normal speech, we often find the uses of ellipses and synecdoques with clear and distinctive purposes.

Ellipses

An ellipsis which serves to illustrate this use, is the one contained in Teolinda's report of her love story, in the Libro Segundo of *La Galatea*. As she composes her narration, Teolinda interjects—by omission—the presence of a previous audience. In so doing, she signals to the new audience that the previous one was not as attentive and as sympathetic to her cause as the group listening to her story now seems to be:

En fin, yo quedé cual ahora estoy, vencida y enamorada, aunque con más confianza de salud que la que ahora tengo. . . . Una cosa me tiene maravillada de cómo cuantas allí estaban no conocieron, por los movimientos de mi rostro, los secretos de mi corazón. (17)

There is a double ellipsis here that is of interest for the themes and the structure that the story of this shepherdes confers on the book. The grammatical ellipsis, "de cuantas (pastoras) allí estaban," leaves out the antecedent shepherdesses. In this omission, the reader's attention is drawn to both the previous group of friends listening to Teolinda, and the present group who reacts more sympathetically. As explained below there are certain functions related to Teolinda's character and speech which are here underlined by her discourse. Consistent with her segmented, elusive appearances, her speech is also marked by ellipses—disgressions, disappearances,

---

(17) *La Galatea*, Book II, p. 69. The elliptical antecedent could be here either *shepherdesses* or *listeners*, however it was left out.

interruptions and connections to other times. As parallel with that of Galatea, her story mirrors the role and nature of the shepherdess' character in the book as a whole. That is, her omissions and flash-backs are consistent with her absence/ presence in the book.

Synecdoques

In the same manner, we find synecdoques of all kinds which are often used in correspondence with the themes centering on the processes of association required by a given character in a certain episode. In the example of Nísida used above ". . . and the desires her grace raised to the loftiest heaven" (pp. 88-9), we have a case in which the abstraction heaven, takes the place of the concrete degree of perfection and interest that Nísida inspires. This example shows how these figures intensify the judgment of aesthetic and moral value applied to the shepherdesses. This applies of course, to whatever other character or subject may be under consideration. Synecdoques using a transposition of a common name for an epithet by which the person becomes an epitome, exceeding in the quality chosen all other persons. These are very common in Cervantes, e.g. [Silviano] *el desamorado* who is more loveless than anyone (18), Camacho, *el rico (Don Quijote)*, and the best known of all Cervantes' characters, "el de la triste figura," and are also used often by Montemayor.

The effect of epitomization, circularity by hyperbole, opposition to lesser beings, and other devices, is important at the syntactic level because of the role they play in stressing

---

(18) For a complete study of the rhetorical figures, their definition and abundant examples from the works of Cervantes see Julio Cejador y Frauca, *La Lengua de Cervantes*, Madrid, Jaime Ratés, two volumes, 1905 especially Vol. I, pp. 519 and ff. See also Keniston's *The Syntax of Castilian Prose: The Sixteenth Century*, already quoted.

or contrasting oppositions, similarities or contrasts at the semantic level, and finally in the total context of the individual work.

These interdependencies are a sort of trademark that is found with constancy in the pastoral narratives. Systematic intention is evident in careful contrivances on the syntactic level, where the continuities of forms can be seen and traced with upmost clarity. And these forms "work" in each of these narratives precisely because they are pastoral conventions. Depending as they do on their self-sufficient aesthetics, they are syntactically, semantically, thematically and generically self-reflective. When mentioning the inner coherence of the genre, I am emphasizing this kind of self-sufficient aesthetic referentiality.

Hyperbaton

Pastoral narrative shows a clear reliance on syntactic forms already used in classical literature as well as in the Neo-Latin productions that were spread throughout Europe by the Italian humanists. One of the most generalized forms purposefully kept in the pastorals is the cultivation of the hyperbaton. This particular syntactic transposition is common in Latin versification and is characteristic of the Virgilian hexameter where the parts of the sentence are displayed in a balanced correspondence.

Nos patriam fugimus; tu, Tityre, lentus in umbra formosam resonare doces Amaryllida silvas (19)

Due to the widespread popularity and authority of Virgil, the rhythm and cadence of this scision of the syntagma

---

(19) Virgil, "Eclogue I": 4-5.

present, in addition to the many possibilities of discontinuous dependencies among the grammatical elements, a case of identity with a form of reputed beauty, an undeniable connection with classical culture.

The hyperbaton adapted so successfully by Petrarch in the vernacular: "Si la mia vita de l'aspero tormento si puo tanto schemire e da gli affanni (20) "became one of the favored syntactic forms, not only in the eclogue and other metered versification, but in the narrative as well. Hyperbaton, which had been favored by earlier Spanish poets such as Juan de Mena (fifteenth century) and further refined and popularized by Fray Luis de León in meditative poetry, was definitely established, with all its possible functions, in the eclogue form by Garcilaso (1503-1536). His third, for instance, begins as an apostrophe that is reminiscent of the way Virgil's shepherds address someone:

> *Aquella voluntad honesta y pura,*
> *ilustre y hermosísima María,*
> *que en mí de celebrar tu hermosura,*
> *tu ingenio y tu valor estar solía. (21)*

Garcilaso also employed it to emphasize the sensorial and expressive value of a sentence:

> *Recoge tu ganado, que **cayendo***
> *de los altos montes las mayores*
> ***sombras**, con ligereza **van corriendo**. (22)*

---

(20) Francesco Petrarca, *Canzoniere*, Sonnet XII, G. Einaudi, Torino, 1958.

(21) Garcilaso de la Vega, *Obras*, Madrid, Espasa-Calpe, Clásicos castellanos, 1961, *Egloga* III, p. 91.

(22) *Ibid., Egloga* II, p. 90. For an interesting analysis of some rhetorical figures in Garcilaso's *Eglogas*, see: Elias L. Rivers, "The Pastoral Paradox of Natural Art," *MLN*, 77 (1962), esp. pp. 132 and 133.

Here and as noted by Garcilaso critics, the distance between *sombras* and *cayendo* has been widened and dramatized by the transposition of the syntactic order and the sense of darkness further stressed by the speed with which the big clouds are literally "running downhill." These and many other functions introduced by Garcilaso were later further explored and re-introduced precisely as part of the appropriate syntax of the language of pastoral (23). In the case of *La Galatea*, for instance the discontinuities of the form often match the development of the episodes (i.e. "Los dos amigos") or act as retardatory devices in the solution of the characters plight (Lenio, Teolinda, Galatea).

Other Stylistic Elements

In addition to syntactic figures, many other devices are used to explore poetic art's ability to create new meanings. The many studies of these devices, however, are largely concerned with the question of sources and influence, while the emphasis here is on the ways these and other possibilities show creativity within the established conventions.

Francisco López Estrada, the most comprehensive analyst of the rhetorical, semantic, and stylistic elements employed by Cervantes in *La Galatea*, mentions the frequent occurrence of pairs of words used for reiteration and balance. These pairings add more than a shade of meaning in a sequence of similar semantic connotation, as for example in "ingrata y desconocida," "lástima y compasión," "disgustos y sinsabores." At times, the pairings also comply with the

---

(23) It has also become a *convention* to repeat that Garcilaso's poetry is so perfect that it resembles natural talk more than poetic speech. His success in blurring the limits between poems and refined oral expression by the measured cultivation of beautiful diction is one of the literary ironies favored in pastoral aesthetics. See the second part of this chapter for a detailed discussion of the pastoral cultivation of seemingly effortless "simple" expression.

principles of internal coherence established in classical literary models, i.e., Ciceronian rules (24).

To this I would add two points. First, it is well known that these linguistic combinations and most of the rhetorical devices—were not innovations of pastoral. They were used well before the sixteenth century; some originated in pre-Hellenistic times (25). The fact that they were used by authors who followed established models indicates that they *worked*, they were efficacious precisely because they were produced, according to well-known rules. In other words, they were conventionalized in compliance with the "vraisemblance" principles of the genre.

Second, the continuity in the use of these devices is necessary for the narration of action and dialogue in pastorals because they act as psychological preparation at the phonetic, syntactic, and semantic levels, creating an "anticipatory" effect. The audiences of pastoral, like the aficionados of any other genre (mysteries, sentimental novels, detective stories), expect these devices as part of their involvement with the work. It would not be "natural," in Culler's terminology (26), to miss these verbal contrivances in the world of the stories they are following with evident interest.

The mediating efforts, as already mentioned, were not exclusive to the Renaissance period nor pastoral narratives alone. Still the point to stress is that the combination of all these features and elements (as well as the alternation prose/

---

(24) Francisco López Estrada, La *"Galatea" de Cervantes: Estudio crítico*, La Laguna de Tenerife, Universidad de La Laguna, 1948, p. 133.

(25) Cf. Aristotle's *Poetics*. See for instance the discussion of the poetic forms used in Tragedy, Comedy (*Dithyrambic*: choral songs [odes] sung in honor of Dyonisus, and *Nomic* poetry, originally concerned with texts taken from the epic and performed accompanied by flute or lyre) 1447a through 1450b, L. Golden and O. Hardison edition, Englewood, N.J., Prentice Hall, 1968, pp. 1-14.

(26) Jonathan Culler, *op. cit., loc. cit.*

verse to be studied below) aim to achieve a coherent fit among the problems presented in the stories, the characters protagonizing the episodes, and the style in which they are expressed.

Without the coherence among the elements, and in the absence of any clear relationship between those rhetorical devices and thematic or structural aims, the harmony is broken, and the work becomes a lifeless exercise. Thus as part of their aesthetic aims, these pastoral narratives abound in rhetorical figures, which serve intensificatory as well as other purposes. As ellipsis can be used for intensificatory rhetorical purposes, so too may other devices be and often are used to either stress a character or a role (such as the quoted "nuevo milagro de hermosura" to emphasize Galatea's role as paragon) or as a delaying tactic in the development of the tale. This is the use and function of some simplificatory devices to be taken up next.

Rhetorical Conventions: Simplification

Emphasis on and hyperbolization of language is not the only way the interaction between the macro-context of knowledge through art and the different micro-contextual levels to manipulate the work is exploited in pastoral aesthetics. The artistic manipulation of rhetorical figures and other grammatical elements is not applied only for intensificatory aims. It is equally exploited for contrastive, oppositional, and simplificatory intentions. For instance, in *Arcadia* from the very beginning there is a determination to show this pleasantness of surroundings through stress on the utter simplicity of expression.

Although the narrator's story is tinged with melancholy, the first part of *Arcadia* is "conventionally idyllic," i.e. beautiful descriptions, discussions and dialogues between the shepherds in the most pleasant tones:

> *Giace nella sommità di Partenio, non umile monte della pastorale Arcadia, un dilettevole piano, di ampiezza non molto spazioso. . . . Ove se io non m'inganno, son forse dodici o quindici alberi di tanto strana ed ecessiva bellezza, che chiunque li vedesse, giudcherebbe che la maestra natura vi si fosse con sommo diletto studiata in formarli. Li quali alquanto distanti, ed in ordine none artificioso disposti, con la loro rarità la naturale bellezza del luogo oltra misura annobiliscono.* (Prosa Prima (27))

From the very beginning the audiences are told that this pastoral story is concerned almost obsessively with simplicity— natural surroundings, simple characters, and in the words of the author, simple styles. For the rustic songs carved on the trees would be as pleasing as those printed in books (28).

That this supposedly unsophisticated poetry is more consistent with the beauty of nature is an idea maintained throughout the entire narrative. It appears and reappears as a "leit-motif" which culminates in the epilogue "A la sampogna" (already the humble instrument of the shepherds in contrast with the flute or fabricated instrument of the court):

> *Il tou umile suono mal si sentirebbe tra quello delle spaventevoli buccine, o delle Reali Trombe . . . [Nè ti curare] . . . , che veramente, se ben pensi, questa è la tua propria e principalissima lode; purchè da' boschi, e da'luoghi a te conventienti non ti diparta.* (29)

---

(27) All quotations of *Arcadia* in the Italian version are taken from Giambattista Corniani, *Arcadia de M. Jacopo Sanazzaro*, annotated by Luigi Portirelli, Milano, Societá Tipografica de' Classici Italiani, 1806.

(28) J. Sanazzaro, *Arcadia*, "Proemio," Portirelli, ed., p. 1.

(29) J. Sanazzaro, *Arcadia*, L. Portirelli, ed., pp. 211 and 213.

But this emphasis on the simplicity, "strana ed ecessiva bellezza," learned from "la maestra natura" ironically emphasizes the artifice involved in the poetic enterprise. The careful selection of the sdrucciulo (30) for the Eclogues in *Arcadia* (just as Virgil had favored the use of the dactylic— _uu—verses because of the versatility they have in stressing various numbers of metric syllables) is made to fit both the sad and melancholic and the grave and elegaic subject, as has been pointed out by other scholars (31).

It is also evident that Sanazzaro, following Boccaccio's metric adaptations such as the ottava rima and the terza rima, as well as Petrarch's influential refinements of the sonnet, is able to compose a narrative of undeniable effect and beauty. His learned command of the subject matter and form does not easily fit into the label of rustic simplicity so often proclaimed in *Arcadia*, and unfortunately just as often taken literally by some critics. The irony that this awareness of the power of language presents is further stressed with the combination of prose and versification in the composition.

The first thing that comes to the reader's attention when dealing with the major pastoral narratives of the Renaissance, —concretely *Arcadia, Los siete libros de la Diana, La Galatea* and *L'Astrée*—is the mixture of prose and metric forms. This holds for lesser pastoral works as well, but an examination of them would take us too far afield in this chapter. The mixture of eclogues and *prosas*, an innovation often attributed to Sanazzaro (32), was in fact first used by Boccaccio in his

---

(30) Esdrújulo: accent on the third from the last syllable; the last two syllables may count as one. Example: "De a/mo/res/e/ter/no/cán/ti/co." Cf. Diego Marín, *Poesía española*, New York, Las Américas, 1962, p. 13 (my translation). Also Luigi Portirelli's annotazioni to *Arcadia*, cited ed., p. 12.

(31) Luigi Portirelli, *op. cit.*, see footnote 30 above.

(32) Giambattista Corniani, "Elogio di M. Jacopo Sanazzaro," in *Arcadia*, Portirelli, ed., p. xv.

Ameto (ca 1320). Since the success of *Arcadia*, it has been taken as the "conventional" or typical form in pastoral narratives of the Renaissance.

The *Arcadia* begins with the gathering of shepherds at the top of Mount Parthenius where they listen to the First Eclogue sung by Ergasto in the form of a complaint with Petrarchan reminiscences. Some days after this episode, Sincero, the narrator, takes to the fields where, meeting with other shepherds, he begins a process of narrative where he is narrator/audience raconteur and acts as listener to the plot.

The explanation/elaboration provided by the prose and the eclogues, and vice versa and what the eclogues illustrate for the stories narrated in prose, allow a number of shifts of pace and tone from the idyllic to the elegaic and political, from the dreamed to the experienced.

After the Fourth Eclogue the pastoral setting is drastically altered with the funeral songs and rites in honor of the deceased Androgeo. In Eclogue 6, the arrival of Carino serves as another "breaking of frame" into a digression that brings to the audience Sincero's life history. In Prosa 8 it is Carino's life that is brought to the intrinsic audience of the story and to the extrinsic audience of the text. But it is precisely these shifts of frame breaking into different idylls or tableaux that permits expansion and treatment of a diversity of aspects (love, mourning, complaints) and a variety of levels (imagined and experienced) with an equal degree of concentrated attention; as if we were putting fragments or scenes of a tapestry under a magnifying glass and moving the glass from scene to scene. This concentration of attention has to be obtained through the special, careful play between the linguistic devices and the compositional combination of forms.

The irony lies in the disclaimers in the *Arcadia* and in *La Galatea* ("there is no tongue able to describe this"). This makes patent pastoral art's dependence on artificiality. This ironic "laying bare" of the sophisticated artistic endeavor through the denial of the effort is another twist in the use of the rhetorical figure known as adynaton and was already exploited by Virgil in his *Eclosgues* (33). And Sanazzaro, who adapted so many of the elements of Virgilian origin, obviously knew this, making the claim to a natural art learned from "teacher nature" even more questionable.

The fact that the lexicon employed throughout *Arcadia* is free from excesses and apparently unaffected should not lead the reader to consider the work as a proof of pastoral's simplicity. This claim itself is a "convention."

> *Tra i quali alcuna volta trovandomi io, e mirando i fronzuti olmi circondati dalle pampinose viti mi corre amaramente nell' animo con angoscia incomparabile, quanto sia lo stato mio difforme da quello degl'insensati alberi, i quali dalle care viti amati dimorano continuamente con quelle in graziosi abbracciari; ed io per tanto spazio di cielo, per tanta longinquità di terra per tanti seni di mare, dal mio desio dilungato, in continuo dolore e lacrime mi consumo.*
> (Prosa Settima (34))

Many other examples could serve to illustrate the point.

Following the rhythm of Sincero's story, it is easy to perceive a number of features of the carefully selected syntax of his account. There is a choice "mise-en-scène" where the speaker can locate himself and compare his wretched situation with that of the happily embracing grapevines climbing up the lofty trees. The comparison is kept in constant balance by the repetition of the pronouns in relation to each

---

(33) Cf. Michael C. J. Putnam, *Virgil's Pastoral Art: Studies in the Eclogues*, Princeton, Princeton University Press, 1970, p. 51, see note 5.

Both Portirelli and Nash document the passages where Sanazzaro's indebtedness to Virgil is clear. The first translation of Virgil's *Bucolics* was the one published by Bernardo Pulci in 1481, and Sanazzaro could have been familiar with it at the time of his writing the different parts of *Arcadia* as well as being familiar with the Latin versions.

(34) J. Sanazzaro, *Arcadia*, Portirelli edition, Prosa Settima, p. 76.

other as well as in relation to the intensifying adverb: "quanto . . . [his emotional state] da quello [of the trees] . . . i
qualle dalle viti . . . con quelle in graziosi abbracciari continu-
amente."

In addition there is a prolongation of his sad "incomparable" state by the repetition, analogically anaphoric, of the
adverbial clauses: "[ed io] per tanto . . . per tanta . . . per
tanti . . . in continuo [dolore] . . ." The rhythm of the linguistic arrangement in Sanazzaro's prose is based more on the
stylistic, syntactic elements than on the sound strata or rhetorical figures of the vocabulary. And it is important to keep
these characteristics in mind, for the eclogues were often
sung or read to the audience and many were represented or
enacted as 'mimes'' (35).

The constant interruption and resumption of the action as
the eclogues and the proses themselves are shifted back and
forth is also relevant. For the audiences, and as in the case of
Tirsi, the sophisticated audiences of the élite court used to
shifts from prose to verse compositions since Boccaccio's
time, these shifts never allow them to forget that they are
listening to and participating in a fictional event.

There is a subtle irony (36) at play, not only because the
readers and listeners are manipulated by the breaking of

---

(35) In addition to Theocritus' Idylls II and X among other well
known "mimes," there were many others that extrapolated from the
conventional themes of shepherd's complaints elaborated on courtly
disquisitions, political arguments, and personal concerns. According to
Greg, the model for the political "mime" of the Renaissance seems to
have been the *Tirsi*, the dramatic eclogue that Castiglione recited in the
year of 1506 before the court of Duke Guidobaldo at Urbino. Cf. W. W.
Greg, *Pastoral Poetry and Pastoral Drama*, London, A. H. Bullen, 1906,
p. 31.

(36) William Empson, who has dealt with pastoral narratives of later
times from a sociological point of view says in this respect: "Irony has
no point unless it is true, in some degree in both senses," that is to say
in the implied and in the expressed sense. See William Empson, *Some
Versions of Pastoral*, Norfolk, New Directions Books, 1950, pp. 55-56.

frame, teased, and prevented from total immersion in the narrative, but because, as Sanazzaro's narrator's voice consistently repeated, the "convention" of the pastoral genre aims at the discussion and treatment of the most complex subjects within an apparent simplicity—of forms, of themes, and of characters. This apparent simplicity is a basic part of the convention—a result of the interplay here between all macro- and micro-contextual elements. It shows the importance of the tension between what is stated by the authors and what is shown when the works are enacted and produced. The enactment makes obvious the role of art and the necessity of the artistic effort (albeit under the guise of effortlessness).

The convention of the eclogue presupposes a world, a society where verbal communication is not only possible, but necessary. The requisite of the eclogue is the communication of personal experiences. The shepherds' art of communication becomes a verbal space where they compete for attention and excellence in the refinement of their feelings and the complex way those feelings are expressed, using concepts and words different from "celles des Bergers ordinaires."

The convention of refined expression of lofty feelings under the ironic disclaimer of simplicity of style and impossibility of expression remained a constant feature of pastoral narratives well into the seventeenth century. It became one of the most durable conventions, although it was maintained with a gradually increasing emphasis on the mastery displayed by the individual authors in exercising this contrivance.

A fitting example of this is found in *L'Astrée* where the almost Ciceronian beauty, style, and harmony of composition betray the repeated denial of refinement:

Mais nous voyons et cognoissons bien aussi que, nous qui, jusques icy, avons mis toute nostre estude à bien aymer, et non pas à le bien dire . . . malaisément pourrons-nous assez bien dire ce que si parfaitement et si religieusement nous avons observé . . . que n'ayant jamais fait autre profession que d'aimer sans le dire, nous serons maintenant bien empêchez de prendre un autre personnage et de recourir aux paroles pour verifier nos actions. (37)

The irony of this "empêchement" is perhaps more pronounced in this work from the seventeenth century after the pastoral dramas, poems and narratives of previous years (particularly Sanazzaro's *Arcadia*, De Ribeiro's *Menina e Moça*, Cervantes' *La Galatea*, and the immensely popular *Diana* of Montemayor) had exploited the conceit, establishing the artistic mediation as a convention.

In addition, the irony manifested with this claim is noticeable in two other ways. First, d'Urfé's audience, the reader or listener who by the fourth chapter was used to the persuasive discourse of the story, was reminded by this denial, of the beauty and perfection of the work. In other words, the author's claim of the lack of art calls attention to the artistry involved. Secondly, for the intrinsic audiences--the shepherds and shepherdesses waiting for their turn to tell and compare their stories—the shift in the narrative acts as a clue for them to begin the appraisal of the expression of feelings and to judge the double-entendre posed by their companion/colleague. From this point of departure, they all become evaluators, interpreters of what is said and of what is implied.

It is not uncommon to find that the same character acts as both speaker and commentator on his/her own discourse (38). One such case is Hylas, one of the shepherds in *L'Astrée*

---

(37) *L'Astrée*, Hugues Vaganay edition, IV, emphasis mine, p. 330.

(38) This durable convention in pastoral narrative, i.e. the raconteur who changes roles—author, narrator, audience, judge, interpreter, observer, onlooker—is one of the features that has remained with peculiar durability in the pastoral narratives and their derivations. Recent examples that come to mind are the figures of Cloverdale in Hawthorne's *The Blithedale Romance* (1852) and Mr. Biswas in Naipaul's *A House*

who tells the audience about one of his experiences, giving an immediate version of the rules (for him) of the game of love:

Elle fuit et fuyant elle veut qu'on l'atteigne:
Refuse et refusant veut qu'on l'ait par l'effort:
Combat et combattant veut qu'on soit le plus fort:
Car ainsi son honneur ordonne qu'elle feigne.

Celui qui n'à pas le courage de vivre de cette sorte,
conseillez luy un autre mestier que celuy d'amour,
car il n'y fera jamais son profit. (39)

Hylas' "madrigal" (40), obviously recited to illustrate one of the many demands imposed by the cult and pursuit of love in their particular pastoral society, is a reminder again of the contrivances involved in art. And it is all the more clear in an art that is dealing with the highest ideas and most intense feelings as if they were a game. Interestingly enough, Hylas, the fickle, is not above calumny against the shepherdesses that reject him. He defines the code of the game of love as the interplay between appearance and truth.

From a formal point of view, the *ritornello* in this *letrilla*, the two-line strophe that usually follows the first group of verses and that serves as a sort of commentary on the preceding stanza, is here in prose form. This integrates the combination of prose-verse so common in this kind of narrative even more. The interplay of micro-contexts and macro-contexts is achieved through a coherence of content and form as well as of stylistic devices that focus the audience's attention on the arrangement and special values of prose and verse.

---

for Mr. Biswas, New York, Penguin Books, 1961. The critic Walter Benjamin deals with the figure of the raconteur (author as artisan) who interprets as in a "praxis." Cf. "The Storyteller" in *Illuminations*, translated by Harry Zohn, New York, Harcourt, Brace and World, 1968.

(39) *L'Astrée*, Hugues Vaganay edition, Book II, p. 116.
(40) According to Jacques Ehrmann, *op. cit.*, p. 13.

In the versified compositions, however, the sound strata, the lexical elements, and the stylistic arrangements within each one of the individual songs or poems are even more important for the necessary coherence among the micro-contexts than they are in the prose selections. This is evident because even when both prose and verse were recited or re-enacted in some way, the rhythmic accent, metric syllables, asonantations, consonantations, and the number of verses involved in the diverse forms of poetry imposes stricter constraints on poetry.

As already discussed in the section of the proceeding chapter dealing with the Italian pastorals, the terza rima and ottava rima had been adopted after Boccaccio's pastoral works as the properly elegant and rustic pastoral meters. For the pastorals of other countries, all the italianate meters were considered elegant while the vernacular forms of versification, especially the ones carried forward from medieval times, were often associated with things less refined. Many of the vernacular forms, however, were also incorporated by the best authors when the episode or the theme was suitable for them. We will see one example of this incorporation in the analysis of *La Galatea* (Chapter VI).

All these poetic and compositional concerns, although not exclusive to pastoral, play an integratory role in the genre not unlike the effect that the "dominant" has within the space of a metric composition. My argument is that the combination, or rather studied shifts from prose to poems (see *L'Astrée* above), even if not exclusive to the pastoral narrative genre, is used in these works to its fullest potential. In switching from prose to verse, the form is so obviously different that the attention of the audience (both intrinsic and extrinsic) is called to a studied and different level of discourse. This enhances the "artificiality" of these compositions even more since no normal (i.e. realistic) situation involves a shift to a poetic declamation. Even if it did—in quotations, voice simulation as in reported speech, or formulae of the various fantasy tales,—the distantiation does not aim at a projection of the personal, individual inner self. The "dedoublements de la personalité" which are "conventional" in pastoral narratives, aim to illustrate the feelings discussed by putting the self of the speaker as paragon, as a reflection on themselves, the storytellers.

The situations represented in pastoral are so "unreal" that the reader/audience is sure to be immersed in a realm separate from the ordinary. Yet these worlds are not totally different from reality since in these works one encounters mountains, rivers, creatures, and even shifts in experience. But the artistic, contrived way those realities or experiences are expressed, where every aspect seems to be a reflection on every other one, makes the audience perceive the distortion, the world-upside-down effect that the poetization creates. Art, in this aesthetic, does not copy reality but imitates in a dream-like form, in a dream that is continuously exposed to appreciation, commentary and judgment by the rest of the members of pastoral society and by the audiences of the stories.

The background of knowledge and the inquiring exercise of the intellect in its pursuit was best conceptualized in the anonymous allegorical political satire *Coplas de Mingo Revulgo* (ca. 1464) where the author—believed to be the historian Hernando del Pulgar—says in the Prologue:

> *Y en esta Bucólica que quiere decir cantar rústico y pastoril, quiso dar a entender la doctrina que dicen so color de la rusticidad que parecen decir; porque el entendimiento, cuyo oficio es saber la verdad de las cosas, se ejercita inquiriéndolas, y goza, como suele gozarse cuando ha entendido la verdad de ellas.* (41)

---

(41) Quoted in Mia Gerhardt, *Essai d'analyse littéraire de la Pastorale dans les littératures italienne, espagnole et française*, The Hague, Van Gorcum, 1950, p. 63.

This quest was already expressed by Virgil in his *Georgics* II, 490: "Felix qui potuit rerum cognoscere causas" and it became one of the macro-contexts for pastoral poetics. In the particular case of the major pastorals of my study, "the intellectual exercise of inquiring about the truth hidden under *rusticity*" which the coplas propose is carried forward by several means. As seen in Chapter III and the present Chapter IV, the search for truth can be accomplished through beauty. Order, the aim and center, hidden beneath chaos and turmoil, can be found by the proper use of *euphemy, decorum discretio*. This search for coherence in a world which seems to be corrupted or decaying is a neo-platonic innovation to which pastoral aesthetics ardently adhered.

The language and rhetorical means were but a part of the process. We will be able to analyze the rest as we face the thematic arguments of these pastoral romances in the next chapter.

CHAPTER V

THEMATIC CONVENTIONS

Even more than in the case of the previously discussed conventions of language and style, thematic conventions used in pastoral works present particular difficulties of definition and classification. The variety and scope of themes in pastoral is vast, almost defying classification. Yet, there have been many attempts to group, define and classify the themes most frequently treated in the different forms of pastoral. From the Idylls and Eclogues, to the romances, poems, pastourelles and dramas, and for all the possible variations of those forms, there have been classificatory perspectives as rich and varied as the thematic topics themselves.

Some approaches which aim at general theories of the implications of the major themes, their definition and classification are found in the works of W. W. Greg, *Pastoral Poetry and Pastoral Drama* (1913), E. R. Curtius, *European Literature and the Latin Middle Ages* (1953), Northrop Frye's *Anatomy of Criticism* (1973), W. Leonard Grant, *Neo-Latin Literature and the Pastoral* (1965), and R. Poggioli, *The Oaten Flute* (1975). Other approaches combine the discussion of themes, historical developments and the comparison of several national literatures to attempt a coherent classification of the genre. Models for such studies are the works of Mia Gerhardt, *Essai d'Analysse littéraire de la pastorale dans les littératures italienne, espagnole et française* (1950) and more recently, that of Helen Cooper, *Pastoral: Medieval into Renaissance* (1977).

Other perspectives also focus on historical developments but concentrate more on the social and cultural situations that surround and condition the manifestations of these pastoral themes. Recent examples of this approach include the works of William Empson, *Some Versions of Pastoral* (1950), Leo Marx, *The Machine in the Garden* (1964), and that of Raymond Williams, *The Country and the City* (1973).

Equally important and productive are the studies that concentrate on the pastoral themes as developed within national literatures. Such are the works of Lèon Levrault, *Le genre Pastoral: Son évolution* (1914) for the pastoral of France, Juan Bautista Avalle-Arce's *La novela pastoril española* (3 vols.; I, 1976, II, 1979) for the pastoral of Spain, James Congleton's *Theories of pastoral poetry in England: 1684-1798* (1952), and Bernard Weinberg's *A History of Literary Criticism in the Italian Renaissance* (1961) for the Italian pastoral, among many others.

Also abundant and important are works that concentrate on individual themes themselves and as developed by individual authors. Among the former are the books by Laurence Lerner, *The Uses of Nostalgia: Studies in Pastoral Poetry* (1972), A. B. Giamatti's *The Earthly Paradise and the Renaissance Epic* (1966), and Daniel Javitch's *Poetry and Courtliness in Renaissance England* (1978) and a vast number of articles, papers, and monographs.

Among the latter are Michael Putnam's *Virgil's Pastoral Art* (1970) and Eleanor Leach's *Virgil's Eclogues: Landscapes of Experience* (1974) on Virgil; López Estrada's *La "Galatea" de Cervantes: Estudio crítico* (1948) on Cervantes and studies on individual works such as Jacques Ehrmann's *Un Paradis désespéré* (1963) and Henri Bouchet, *L'Astrée,*

*ses origines, son importance dans la formation de la littéra-
ture classique* (1923) on *L'Astrée.*

The above are indispensable for my study. Without this
body of scholarship, an analysis of the integration of some
representative pastoral conventions in the major narratives
of the Renaissance would be impossible. I will neither review nor dispute theoretically what has already been said.
Rather I will provide a fresh examination of the way the
great Renaissance pastoral prose romances (1) established a
particular kind of aesthetics.

The authors of these romances appropriated words, expressions, and themes successfully used in other works of the
genre by masters of both classical and contemporary fame.
By this re-appropriation, these authors both gave form to literary fantasies and engaged their audience in an intellectual
game involving both playfulness and textual recognition.
Through these activities, these authors constructed worlds
that never were, times that could not exist, and produce feelings of love of an intensity otherwise unattainable.

Tracing the genealogies of elements in the pastoral is a
nearly endless task and so I limit my attention to a few universal themes, knowing that other possibilities exist (2). Con-
centrating on the artistic manipulations involved in fashioning these models, I analyze the literary conventions as tools
of artistic invention which then are used to mirror reality.

---

(1) Because these books are different from the novel genre as it developed after *D. Quixote*, there is a great deal of confusion when describing them. Peter Marinelli uses this interesting definition in his *Pastoral*, London, Methuen and Co., 1971, p. 28.

(2) For analyses of the pastoral model as a political reflection of society, see Raymond Williams, *The City and the Country*, Oxford, Oxford University Press, 1973. Renato Poggioli in *The Oaten Flute: Essays
on Pastoral Poetry and the Pastoral Ideal* also touches on the political
implications and critiques of pastorals such as Tolstoy's *War and Peace*,
Goethe's *Faust*, Shakespeare's *As You Like It*, Cervantes' *Dialogue of
the Dogs*, and George Crabbe's *The Village*, among others. See especially pages 29-39.

This chapter begins with analysis of the interrelationships between the themes and their expression as they in turn reproduce similar themes and expressions of earlier texts. An exploration of the author/audience/intertextuality as it is expressed through the themes of Fortune, Time, Love, and Nature in the narrative pastorals of my study follows that. The last part integrates the main themes as they relate to and are framed by melancholy.

Conventional Themes and Creative Intertextuality

Literary productions have consistently provided effective formulas within which the universal problems of existence are represented and examined. Because of their emphasis on fictionality and literariness, pastoral works represent a unique attempt to address eternal human concerns. The poetic bases of the pastoral narratives consist of conscious and studied reappropriations of the language and themes used by well-known authors in widely-known works of the genre; that is, they rest on interweaving present themes with recaptured themes and rhetorical achievements of the past. As a result, pastoral works not only respond to the demands of a given aesthetic (i.e. the way these authors have organized their thoughts and given expression to particular kinds of experience) but also, are attempts to achieve an identification with a particular way of dealing with essential human concerns by linguistic means. They face changeless problems by using unchanged language. Of course, there is a paradox for these eternal concerns—the inexplicable power of Fortune in human affairs, the mysteries of unceasing Time, and the uncontrollable forces that seem to rule human Love--are in fact all subject to change. And the very act of literary appropriation itself involves change.

These subjects are so inextricably related in these works that they appear in all instances united in a chain of themes. In it, Love, Fortune, and Time are the cornerstones that condition the characters' state of melancholy, and reciprocally, their melancholic state is the reason that they are often unable (unless they employ discretion) to balance their passions against external powers.

This is, for example, how the chain of themes is introduced at the beginning of the Primero Livro of *La Diana*:

> *Baxaba de las montañas de León el olvidado Sireno a quien Amor, la Fortuna, el Tiempo, tratavan de manera que del menor mal que en tan triste vida padecía, no se esperaba menos que perdella. . . . Consideraba aquel dichoso tiempo que por aquellos prados y hermosa ribera apacentaba su ganado poniendo los ojos en solo el interesse (sic) que de traelle bien apacentado se le seguía.* (3)

This unrequited Sireno, upon whom Love, Fortune, and Time seem to have turned their backs, takes refuge in the remembrance of a happier time when his only cares were watching the sheep, contemplation of the beautiful countryside, and composition of songs for which he always received high praise.

The audience finds this melancholic shepherd in the midst of a conventionally perfect landscape, singing and remembering a moment of happiness now gone. But his meditation and remembrances do not last long. Immediately after his song, he engages in a lengthy and highly poetic dialogue with one of his closest shepherd-friends. Whether in the solitude of his meditations, the composition of his verses or the conversations with his friends, the subject and interest constantly dis-

---

(3) Jorge de Montemayor, *Los Siete Livros de la Diana*, Madrid, Espasa-Calpe, Clásicos castellanos, 1967, pp. 9-10.

cussed are the same themes of Fortune, Time, and ephemeral Love.

What is the actual formula that pastoral literature provides for the expression of these fundamental concerns? Pastoral narratives comprehend a double aim: to promote a more refined kind of literature and to integrate it within an artistic tradition. The medium employed to express the identification with other voices of the past and to portray the themes they share is a continual verbal exteriorization. All characters of these pastoral novels arrange emotional episodes of their lives and report them in narration. Both the intrinsic listeners of the stories and the extrinsic audiences of the texts never see their actual actions, but reported versions of the things that happen to them. The front or outside narrator is disguised as a character in a play or staged scene whose words frame, introduce, and condition the actions that are presented to the audience as the true, intimate reality.

This how the shepherds of the First Eclogue are introduced in Sanazzaro's *Arcadia:*

> *Ergasto solo, senza alcuna cosa dire or fare, a piè d'un albero dimenticato de sè e de' suoi greggi giaceva . . . del cui misero stato Selvaggio mosso a compassione, per darglie, alcun conforto, così amichevolmente ad alta voce cantando gl' incominciò a parlare.* (Prosa Prima)

> *Selvaggio:*
>   *Ergasto mio, perchè solingo e tacito*
>   *Pensar ti veggio? oimè, che mal si lasciano*
>   *la pecorelle andare a lor ben placito* (Egloga Prima (4))

The narrator sets the scene and reports how the shepherd, in solitude (in a state of *otium* and *dimenticato de se*) has

---

(4) Jacopo Sanazzaro, *Arcadia*, Luigi Portirelli edition, Milano. Società Tipografica De' Classici Italiani, 1806, Egloga Prima, p. 6.

achieved a distance from which a complicated literary scheme is constructed. Both the *olivadado* Sireno and the *solo* Ergasto, like the Virgilean Tityrus sitting under the idyllic beech tree and the melancholic Cyclops of Theocritus looking over the cliff are brought to the audiences by way of verbal exteriorization. That is, by telling their stories to others.

The shepherds in the above examples are poet/performers, involved either voluntarily or at the supposed request of their audience in singing or reciting their compositions. Their melancholic state, their distance from the present is a thematic leit-motiv. With the help of memory, they revisit a past time when they were happier.

But the convention of thematic distance also points to the linguistic and rhetorical bases of these pastoral fictional realities. They are nostalgic about the past and they sing and use the language of authors of the past. Sireno's audiences—both the internal one (the sympathetic nymphs) and the external one (the readers of the text)—encounter the words of his songs and the themes related with an awareness different from that created in other kinds of literary works. This awareness is conditioned by a purposeful re-elaboration of the themes and words employed by earlier authors.

In the Seventh Book of *La Diana*, the shepherd Arsileo, thinking that he has lost his beloved Belisa forever and not knowing that she is nearby searching for him, sings a song at the request of some shepherds. The stage-like scene is arranged in preparation for the song:

> [*Ella*] *verdadermente pensó lo que veya ser alguna visión o cosa de sueño. Y estando atenta, vio cómo el pastor començó a tocar el rabel tan divinamente, que parecía cosa del cielo; y aviendo tañido un poco con una voz más angélica que de hombre humano, dio principio a esta canción:*

I

¡Ay vanas esperanças, quántos dïas
anduve hecho siervo de un engaño
y quán en vano mis cansados ojos
con lágrimas regaron este valle!
pagado me an amor y la fortuna
pagado me an, no sé de qué me quexo.

1/2/3/4/5/6

II

Gran mal devo passar, pues yo me quexo
que hechos a sufrir están mis ojos
los trances del amor y la fortuna;
¿sabéis de quién me agravio? de un engaño
de una cruel pastora deste valle
do puse por mi mal mis tristes ojos.

6/3/5/2/4/3

III

Con todo mucho devo yo a mis ojos
aunque con el dolor, dellos me quexo
pues vi por causa suya en este valle
la cosa más hermosa que en mis dïas
jamás pensé mirar y no me engaña
pregúntelo al amor y a la fortuna.

3/6/4/1/2/5

IV

Aunque por otra parte la fortuna
el tiempo, la ocasión, los tristes ojos
el no estar receloso del engaño
causaron todo el mal de que me quexo

y assi pienso acabar mis tristes dĭas
cantando mis passiones a este valle.

5/3/2/6/1/4

V

Si el rĭo, el soto, el monte, el prado, el valle,
la tierra, el cielo, el hado, la fortuna,
las horas, los momentos, años, dĭas,
el alma, el corazón, también los ojos,
agravian mi dolor quando me quexo
¿porqué dizes, pastora, que mengaño ? [sic]

4/5/1/3/6/2

VI

Bien sé que me engañé, mas no es engaño,
porque de aver yo visto en este valle
tu estraña perfición, jamás me quexo
sino de ver qué quiso la fortuna
dar a entender a mis cansados ojos
que allá vernĭa el remedio, tras los dĭas.

2/4/6/5/3/1

E

· ·
Canción, de amor y de fortuna quexo
y pues duró un engaño tantos dĭas
regard ojos, regard el soto, el valle. (5)

6/1/4

Since this song is heard by a shepherdess who, unbeknownst to the singer, is hiding nearby, there are at least three audiences. The most immediate one is the shepherdess; the

_____
(5) Jorge de Montemayor, *op. cit.*, Livro Quinto, pp. 231-232.

second, the commentator who reports the lines of the singer, and third, the readers of the text. It could also be that a reader, taking the voice of the narrator, is reading these stories to yet another external audience. Whether this *"lesse-drama-"* like activity takes place or not, is merely speculation on my part. I cannot take my hypothesis any further. There are moments, however, when an audience larger than an individual reader seems to be the target of the text. This is the case in some of the dialogical and eclogue-like songs, in the episodes where riddles are played, and in some kinds of debates among the characters.

Whether reading or listening to these lines, the audience of *La Diana* is treated to a number of literary experiences that are both familiar and unique to pastoral works; specifically the obvious manipulation of conventions. First, readers (or listeners) would immediately recognize the parallel, almost mirror repetition that the words of the *sestina* echo from the Canción that Diana herself sang in the Primero Livro of the Book:

> Ojos que ya no veys quien os mirava
> quando érades espejo en que se vïa
> ¿qué cosa podreys ver que os dé contento?
> Prado florido y verde, do algún dïa
> por el mi dulce amigo yo esperava,
> llorad comigo el grave mal que siento. (6)

The themes of the eyes, weary eyes victims and causes of deceit, vehicles of love, subjects of the whims of Fortune, represent for the reader one more elaboration of those themes in the context of the romance. They are thus, consistent *vraisemblable* with the main and recurrent themes that form the axis of the book.

---

(6) Jorge de Montemayor, *op. cit.*, Primero Livro, p. 24.

Second, readers or listeners to the *sestina* alone—as in this case as an example of Montemayor's art—will be equally engaged by a special literary experience, by the persuasion of the repetition, the multiple directions, the intellectually exciting game of words that the sextine structure requires. Thus the echo of the six words of the verse endings: días (1)/engaño (2)/ojos (3)/valle (4)/fortuna (5)/quexo (6)/stay in the mind of the audience as notes in the phrases of a musical composition linger providing the association of ideas and sound.

The echo effect is here realized not only because of the synthesis provided by the *congedo* (7) (the tercet that serves as "envoy" of the six free-rhymed stanzas), but because, given the choice of concepts involved, these six words can be freely arranged by the ear in a variety of ways, most of them with syntactic meaning of their own. One could take, for instance, the word-endings of the fourth stanza: fortuna/ojos/engaño/quexo/días/valle [Fortune (to my) eyes (caused deceit, (I) complain (all my) days (in this) valley] and that sequence would summarize one of the main themes of *La Diana*, and by extension, of all pastorals. This is the shepherd's eternal complaint that Fortune has caused his eyes to be deceived by the illusion of a Love that is impossible or that is not for him. And this is what the lines have been repeating in one order or another throughout the composition as a whole.

The phonetic and conceptual play of words, as a characteristic trait of the sextine form, is further emphasized in this particular case by the fact that this is a double sextine, arranged in almost (8) identical double structure to reproduce

---

(7) From congé (Fr.) "a formal permission to depart, dismissed, leave-taking, farewell. *Webster's Third New International Dictionary of the English Language*. Unabridged, Springfield, Mass., Merriam-Webster, 1961.

(8) See description and origins of the sextine in Chapter III, fn. 48. This sextine has an irregular second stanza. It repeats the same word-ending *ojos* twice and therefore the word *días* has been omitted. When referring to this particular sextine, I call it a *sestina* following the Spanish usage.

and to echo what was being said throughout. The repetitions, multiple directions, and associations manipulated in these all prose or verse compositions are obviously intentional.

The linguistic and formal schemes used in these pastoral works cannot be considered as isolated examples of some conventional or imitative exercise. Being part of total contextual works, the rhetorical and linguistic schemes are used as a function of the choice of themes. That is to say, there is in these pastoral texts a correspondence between the things to be told, and the words and forms that tell it—between what is to be said and how it is said. As the pastoral characters (and by implication, authors) express their concerns and problems competing for the best way to convey their personal stories, the stories in turn become a premeditated form of text. In it, by means of analogies, hyperboles, similarities, parallels, and studied contrasts, the audience is persuasively taken into a field of contextual and inter-textual associations in an elegant literary game that is entertaining and instructive. Thus encountering a new Tirsi, a beautiful Galatea, or another version of the unrequited Damon, the readers/audiences will have grounds for recognizing those characters by associating them with the qualities and roles that belong with those names.

There is a necessary display of knowledge and of skill by both authors and audiences; skill in intermeshing themes already chosen as proper conventions of the genre and display of knowledge because those themes have to be properly reelaborated as part of a total intertextual scheme. My point is that the audiences of pastoral cannot be considered as passive; they have to respond to the challenge of the game of rhetorical and thematic recognition played by the authors.

Sixteenth century followers of the pastoral genre (and the popularity of these prose romances attests that there were many) (9) would be involved in the themes and expressions used in Montmayor's *sestina* in a way not very different from the way the authors were involved when elaborating their works. That is to say, by their own admission (10), authors were in close communication with the intended readers of their works, a point I will elaborate later. Equally important, they are all in a dialectical relationship with a background of works of the genre in a web of intertextuality. This is demonstrated by the strong emphasis on the appropriation and re-elaboration of conventions from earlier texts and is particularly obvious in the fusion of the main pastoral themes.

Read in comparison with others of his *sestina*—for instance, the regular six-stanza of Livro Segundo in the same work *La Diana* (Aguas que de lo alto desta sierra/baxais con tal ruido al hondo valle), Montemayor's *sestinas* is one of many variations that give a consistent pastoral character to his work. And the connections suggested by all the themes and forms used point to a wider intertextual field. The words of Montemayor's shepherd "and how in vain my weary eyes/with their tears have filled this valley" give the educated audiences of pastoral a clue that they should associate this sestina with similar words and themes in other pastorals.

In *Arcadia's* Egloga Quarta, for instance (Chi vuol udire i mei sospiri in rime/ Donne mie care, e l'angoscioso pianto . . . Ben mille notte ha gia passate in pianto, tal che quasi paludi ho fatto i campi" (11). Having the shepherd express those words in a sextine format gives the audiences an addi-

---

(9) *La Diana* first published in 1559 (in Valencia?) and then in 1560 in Zaragoza was reprinted continuously until 1662 by all the important presses of Europe and translated again regularly until 1750 (Hamburg) into all the major languages. *La Galatea* was also widely read and translated. A version in French was published in 1783 by Jean-Pierre Claris de Florian, nephew of Voltaire with the title *Estèlle*.

(10) See Chapter III for declarations on this matter, such as d'Urfé's introduction and Virgil's address to the Consul (audience) in Eclog. IV.

(11) Jacopo Sanazzaro, *op. cit.*, Egloga Quarta.

tional clue to associate these words with the words used in similar metric compositions of other pastorals. The word-pattern is as powerful a nexus as the themes in these games of literary association. Thus the words of the melancholic Arsildo (valle, quexa, ojos, días) repeat the theme of complaint and melancholy he finds in his situation, a situation typical of the clichéified *lacrimarum valle* of the shepherds of Sanazzaro and others. And being repeated six times twice by the requirements of the form, his voice acts as another instrument, or another singer's voice in the total harmony-like concert of pastoral. Different voices repeat similar words in endless variations of one, or many themes.

There are many other possibilities in this reappropriation of earlier masters' words. Themes such as the eyes filling the country with the sentimental tears of the literary shepherds can be and were associated with many similar themes and works of the past. Spanish audiences, for instance, could associate Arsildo and Elpino's words with those of Nemoroso in Garcilaso's *Egloga I* ("yo hago con mis ojos/ crecer, llovidendo, el fruto miserable"). And educated audiences would have no trouble in recognizing the dialogical character of Egloga Quarta as an echo of Virgil's VII where Corydon and Tyrrenus (12) express their unrequited passions in similar alternating songs.

One could conclude from the borrowing, repeating, and reappropriating of conventions that the pastoral contains intentions other than the merely aesthetic and entertaining. That is, in addition to entertaining and pleasing, the activity connects the audiences and the texts to earlier audiences and earlier literary products. The amount of scholarship dedicated to this subject is staggering (13) and has clarified many

---

(12) Tirreno and Albanio are the protagonists of Garcilaso's *Egloga III.*

(13) Examples of those studies are William Empson's *Some Versions of Pastoral*, Norfolk, New Directions Books, 1950, and Raymond Williams's *The Country and the City*, cited above.

implications related to art and social conditions, art and the consumer, and even the manipulation of the audiences for various purposes.

My own attention is directed here to some aspects related to art, the artist, and the communication with the reader (audience) specifically, the quest for conscious author-reader participation. In a synchronic way, the author's mode of address to the selected and pre-selected implied audience is evident in the books' dedicatories to patrons and princes. Some of those patrons and friends, thinly disguised under "pastoral" names, were later included in the plot of the books either as characters or as objects of laudatory addresses. Examples of these incipient *romans-à-clef* are Montalvo's *El Pastor de Fílida*, Sidney's *Arcadia*, and many sections of *La Diana, La Galatea* and *L'Astrée,* among others.

But the question of author-audience participation takes on implications extending far beyond synchronic direct communication. On the one hand, the very activity of appropriating successful conventions from the past underscores the need of literature to work within a literary context. And this is necessary for both the production and for the understanding of the many nuances and characteristics of literary art. On the other hand, the repetition of these conventions illuminates the fact that art is not totally subject to historical determinism. This is, in my view, one of the major ironies of pastoral works and one of their most interesting aspects. The circumstances existing when they were produced have changed; many aspects of style have changed too. Yet subsequent audiences are able to feel affinity with the problems expressed through those themes and words and can also enjoy the intricacies of the books. Though contemporary audiences are not really able to guess if a given member of the court or a famous poet is hidden under a particular "pastoral name," we can recognize the themes of unsynchronized love, of dispossession, melancholy, and nostalgia that form the core of these novels; and we are thus able to enjoy the familiar adventures. All of these themes have in fact been re-adapted countless times: Arsildo's love triangle in Valera's *Pepita Jiménez*; Céladon, the almost epic hero of Love, in many soap operas and movies; and the musical quality of the eclogues and songs are by now one more link in the texture of our cultural background.

Contemporary studies have re-opened the problems and questions posed by the demands of the conscious author-reader participation which is so important in pastoral aesthetics. The works of Hans R. Jauss, Georg Lukács, Manfred Naumann, and others (e.g. the Frankfurt School) attest to the enormous interest of these issues for literary criticism and for the understanding of literature.

Addressing this issue, Peter Hohendahl argues that the evocative power of past works of art constitutes an important theoretical challenge for literary criticism to meet. At the heart of this is the process by which a past work is pulled out of the flow of time and made part of the present. He suggests that historicity of literary works might best be understood as the ability to be made "present" many times over (14).

The authors of the masterpieces of pastoral interweave conventional (i.e. similar) efforts and conventional words that appear clichéified, but ironically, these seemingly unchangeable forms and words provide an effective vehicle for dealing with eternal problems, eternal themes. Perhaps a reminder is necessary here that only those authors who truly are capable of the creativity required in the process of work concretization can achieve permanence or endurance. Imitators, followers of the *letter* of the convention, only produce lifeless copies which cannot withstand the changes of lifestyles and of literary tastes.

---

(14) Peter U. Hohendahl, Introduction to Reception Aesthetics, *New German Critique*, Bloomington, Indiana University Press, 1977, p. 54.

The forces of love, fortune, time, and nature, acting here in artistic (fictional) societies, not only have to be presented through the idiom of conventional language and rhetorical forms, but these linguistic and rhetorical conventions have to be elaborated so that they interact among themselves and with the themes that they express. Concepts and themes interact with the means of expression and thus condition the texture and action of the narratives. Fortune, time, love, and nature thus become the constant leif-motif of these pastoral novels. Complete documentation of all the instances reflecting these particular theme/language interactions would be too lengthy, but a few examples will illustrate the point.

The introductory words of *La Diana* have already been quoted. "Baxaba de las montañas de León el olvidado Sireno a quien Amor, la fortuna, el tiempo, tratavan de manera que del menor mal que en tan triste vida padecía, no se esperaba menos que perdella." These words are found again and again in the monologues, dialogues, songs and conversations of all the characters of the book. "Yo confesé que avía querido bien, porque el amor, quando es verdadero, no sufre cosa encubierta (15). "¿Qué harémos, hermosa señora, a los golpes de la fortuna? ¿Qué casa fuerte avrá adonde la persona pueda estar segura de las mudanças del Tiempo?" (16).

These concerns are, of course, not only the matter of *La Diana* alone. Says Céladon, responding to the requests of Léonide, one of his many admirers in *L'Astrée*: "Belle nymphe, entre tous les plus misérables, je me puis dire le plus rigoureusement traité de la fortune, car pour le moins ceux qui ont du mal ont aussi permission de s'en doulor. . . .

---

(15) Jorge de Montemayor, *op. cit.*, "Carta de Don Felis para Celia," p. 117.
(16) *Ibid.*, "Las nymphes a Diane," p. 123.

-Quand j'ai dit cela, répondit Astrée, j'ai parlé selon mon humeur, et selon ma passion, et je vous assure que la résolution que j'en ai faite n'est pas moins irrévocable que les Arrêts de la fatalité" (Septième Partie) (17).

Similar sentiments about the unfair treatment by fortune and the consequences of love were sung by the mysterious young hermit in the "Primero Libro de Galatea": "Si han sido el cielo, amor y la fortuna,/ sin ser de mí ofendidos,/ contentos de ponerme en tal estado/ en vano al aire envío mis gemidos" (18). Love, fortune, and time are thus considered not only as feelings and experiences but also as conventions used to explain essential causes that affect the lives and destinies of all humans.

Considered as essential causes, these elements—Love, Fortune, and Time—often act as independent characters with their own reasons for existing. Their purpose is to highlight the gap between the essences toward which all moves in this neo-Platonic search and the confusion and defective nature of the empirical experiences. This is evident in La Diana, Galatea, L'Astrée, as the above examples illustrate. By the continuous repetition in these themes, the importance of the conflict between human and external forces is reinforced and the adoption of these debates, as required by the conventions of this genre, is further justified.

In the above, Elpino and Ergasto in Arcadia, Arsileo in La Diana, the hermit of La Galatea, and Céladon in L'Astrée find themselves in similar predicaments as a consequence of uncontrollable chains of events (Fortune) via the unceasing change of Time, because they are patients/ victims of some unbalanced passion meeting Love as an antagonist, a force out of personal control. The contrast between the joy of their moment of love (love as an absolute experience) and the wretchedness of their present situation is the result of un-

---

(17) L'Astrée, Genette ed., pp. 60-63.
(18) La Galatea, cited edition, Primer Libro, pp. 122-123.

graspable, unceasing change. This in turn produces the feeling of melancholy and the overwhelming nostalgia to return to the attainment of Love. In other words, the tension occurs because there is a great discrepancy between the immutability of the essences and the changeability of the human experiences. Time and Love as essential concepts that we conceptualize seem evermore unattainable in the fluidity of events. Two examples, one from *La Diana* and one from *L'Astrée* illustrate this point.

As in many other instances in the book two shepherds, Sylvano and Selvagia discuss the means to end the torment of unrequited love as they talk, set against the "natural" background of an idyllic milieu:

Silvano:
> — *¿Y esso [el amor] podrías tu acaballo contigo?--dixo Silvano.*

> — *Como la fortuna o el tiempo lo ordenase—respondió Selvagia.*

> — *Aora te digo—dixo Silvano muy admirado—que no te aria agravio en no aver manzilla de tu mal porque el amor que está subjecto al **tiempo** y a la **fortuna**, no puede ser tanto que dé trabajo a quien lo padece.* (19)

In this idyllic retreat where the casuistics of love are laid out and related to the other thematic forces the shepherdess defends the power of those forces (external characters) which seem to be in control: "As fortune or time would command" she says. The "unrequited" Sireno sees love as a personal problem because he is experiencing it as an empirical sentiment. "Now I can say to you, responded Silvano with amazement, do not feel offended if I do not agree with the depth

---

(19) Montemayor, *op. cit.*, Livro Segundo, pp. 68, 69. Emphasis mine.

of your sorrow, for Love that is dependent on Time and Fortune cannot be so great that it would burden the lover" (20). Love is a burden for him not because of the passion itself but because of the changes that time in progress, the fluidity of events, has brought to his situation and feelings.

The view of the theme of Love as an independent actor proving its might and even operating at times as an antagonist to the character is repeated almost as a leit-motiv in *L'Astrée*. Says for instance Céladon:

> *Et toutefois il sembla qu'Amor, pour montrer sa puissance, voulut expressément de personnes tant ennemies en unir deux si étroitement, que rien n'en peut rompre les liens que la mort.* (21)

Love, like Fortune and Time, for the shepherdesses of these pastorals appears as an archetypical, independent force or pattern, against which the unpredictable, fluid, and changeable course of human events (including experiences of love) has to be measured. But it is at the level of the human experience that these dramas take place. In this sense that the themes of Love, Time, Fortune are exploited in these pastorals as conventions which will serve as contrasts between the ideal-imagined and the real-empirical.

---

(20) With this refutation, the author deftly saves his argument from the possible attack and censure of the Index which had fallen on others in and out of Spain. Américo Castro ("Erasmo en tiempo de Cervantes," en *Hacia Cervantes*, Madrid, Taurus, 1960) states in note 3, p. 195:

> "*Sabido es que la Congregación del Indice, fuera de España, censuró a Montaigne, Lipsio, Maquiavelo y G. Bruno por decir que el mundo está gobernado por la fuerza ciega del destino y por abusar de la palabra fortuna.*" (Véase F. Strowski, *Pascal et son temps*, p. 54).
> (21) d'Urfé, *op. cit.,* Genette ed., Première Partie, p. 63.

Rules of Love

To provide a pattern to guide the conduct of the lovers, formalized rules are given and discussed constantly in these works. These rules, based on the Neo-Platonic cult of love and conventionalized after Petrarchean models, are best summed up in the famous Douze Tables des Lois d'Amour in *L'Astrée*. Two examples from those Tables are especially representative of my point: "Only he who can lose in the Extreme is the perfect lover. Mediocrity deserves treason and not fidelity" (Première Table). A stricter rule has to be followed if one is to find perfect love:

Onzième Table

Que la perte de raison,
Que les liens et la prison,
Pour elle en son âme il chérisse.
Et se palise à s'y renfermer
Sans attendre de son service
Que le seul bonheur de l'aimer (22)

In spite of the laws and the effort to make everyone follow the right norms of behavior (that is to say, to approximate as much as possible the concept of perfect Love), the variety of characters, the nuances of similar feelings and the inexorability of the changes of Fortune and Time make these rules impossible to maintain. As each of the tales show, when the members of these pastoral societies try to maintain them, problems occur because there is seldom a perfect balance (*decorum*) either in intensity—as Astrée had pointed out earlier, his offense was unbalanced love ("l'offense qu'il m'avait faite n'etait procédée que de m'aimer trop")—or due to the complications of the lack of synchronization be-

---

(22) *Ibid.*, Deuxième Partie, p. 120.

tween their passions or feelings. Galatheé, Sylvie, and Léonide love Céladon who, in turn, is in love with Astrée. Lycidas and Hylas (who pursues many shepherdesses including Astrée) love her but Astrée cannot love anyone but Céladon. Astrée's and Céladon's passion, alas, is impossible because of circumstances (Fortune) that lie beyond their control.

Thus the action that these narratives present implicates a large number of characters in constantly conflicting amorous situations. The problem underscored with these shifts is not so much one image of perfect love—either as agape (friendly love) or as Eros (physical love) but the fluidity of human love itself.

The individual stories of Astrée, Céladon, Sincero, Diana, and the countless shepherds of these narratives have a shape and a drama of their own. Presented as vignettes—eclogues in the sense of small episodes, *ex logos*, outside the discourse within the narrative—these stories are dominated each by the central personality which represents a point of view, an aspect or side in this elegant literary game. These aspects are not only conflictful and philosophical but, by the very nature of the effort to present the multifaceted themes of love, they include the humorous, the serious, and even the titillating.

Such are the episodes in which Céladon, disguised as a woman and under a female pseudonym, shares a bedroom with a young nymph and the similar case of Ysmenia in the First book of *La Diana* who also enjoys, under a disguise, all degrees of amorous ambiguities. In a more serious and almost tragic vein, the story of Timbrio and Silerio—"Los dos amigos"—in *La Galatea* involves the theme of friendship being tested and surrendering to the pressure of Love. Thus the conflicts and variations on the theme of love which make most of the substance of the pastoral stories not only represents a major Neo-platonic philosophical preoccupation but also a source of interesting and entertaining reading for the audiences of the pastoral genre. Nor is the variety and diversity of the experiences contrary to abstraction and generalization of experience, for generalization can be derived from the multiple cases. The effort to enumerate and classify this diversity is an attempt to arrive at a coherent, general abstraction which will serve as the model to explain them all.

The same prevailing fascination with the attempt to grasp the mysteries of love affects the shepherds' concern with the durability of the feelings (eternity), even though their discourses contain an almost obsessive awareness of time. Because of this awareness, the idyllic episodes in their pre-arranged completeness represent an attempt to take refuge in a time, a moment that can be encapsulated, kept for analysis and scrutiny. To do so, they elaborate as models, events and situations of a time past (Golden moments).

But there is a dilemma and contradiction in this attempt to stop and immobilize the change. The unchangeable perfection that the "Première Table" of the Laws of love, proposes, amounts to the impossibility of change, and ultimately to total annihilation—even of the passion of Love which the Laws seek to preserve. In pastoral attempts to grasp immutability, there is an anxiety almost identical to that underscored in the Socratic inquiry on the nature of language. Language, as the *Cratylus* repeatedly states, is in constant change, and Time is often perceived as an unpredictable continuum. Yet the segmented—idyllic and idealized—stories of these pastorals are told as organized (i.e. predictable) interruptions of the continuities that we perceive as real life. Thus for pastoral, Time is not only one of the basic thematic concerns but a major linguistic and philosophical concern as well.

As in all literary fictions, the dilemma faced by pastoral art is that the shepherds' stories with their reported episodes, shepherd's complaints, songs, ironic and hyperbolic statements, verses and singing matches are creations of language and, as such, they are also events in time. Pastoral stories, in addition, use themes that involve the actions of a past time, using the language of past authors and identifying with the situations of characters of past fictions. The aesthetics of the genre require this coherence among the language and the themes as a convention in order to maintain a special degree of aesthetic *decorum*, to respond to the rules of *vraissemblance*. In the books selected for my analysis, there are many instances where the themes, language, and rhetoric are perfectly fused, and these represent masterpieces of the aesthetics of the genre.

The story of Carino in *Arcadia*'s Prosa 8 with its re-elaboration of Virgil's Eclogues V, VII, and X is a good representative example of my point. Trying to console Sincero and to bring him out of his state of melancholy, Carino recounts the story of his own similar predicament (23).

The story narrated by Carino is told in a brief interlude of the shepherd's day. During this brief period, the complete story of the five days in the life of the shepherd is narrated. Time thus can be condensed, limited, or framed by verbal arrangement. This is what Lowry Nelson, in reference to the uses of time in poetry calls "narrative time" or "The time in which the narration or performance takes the place of the time which is narrated or implied" (24).

But if time can be condensed, the opposite is also true here. If the story of five days can be condensed in one afternoon, then this afternoon is timeless. Only the verbal speed of the character and the texture or number of his added details limit the actual timespan. In the hands of the storyteller, time becomes something that expands or contracts. In the pastoral tales, the time narrative, molded by the author and performed by the shepherd's voice, has expanded by way of the verbal tenses, not only to a recent past ("When immoderately desirious of dying [he] went to a towering cliff") but

---

(23) Cf. Sanazzaro, *op. cit.*, Portirelli, Prosa Ottava, pp. 92-95.
(24) Lowry Nelson, *Baroque Lyric Poetry*, New Haven, Yale University Press, 1961, p. 39.

by way of the most persuasive use of the "historical present tense" when he addresses her in the vocative: ("See how you win at last"), thus bringing to the scene a much more distant past ("When [they] went through the woods together gathering the ruddy strawberries").

An additional use of the time element distinguishes pastoral poetics from any other and makes the pastoral time segmentation unique. Because of the convention of quoting other authors, borrowing their sentences, names, and sayings as if making literary découpages, the time span of these stories is truly a literary time. When the shepherd calls his forsaking nympth: "O crudelissima ed a' miei preghi più sorda che gl'insani mormorii dell'enfiato mare," and reminds her of the time when they gathered flowers and fruits of the fields, the audience is not only taken to a past time but to the literary, textual time of the Idylls of Theocritus, the Eclogues of Virgil, and the countless identical episodes repeated in all pastorals. The story of Carino is in fact a re-elaboration of the theme taken up by Virgil in Eclogues V (the death of Daphnis), VIII (unrequited young love of the shepherd and Damon), and X (the attempted suicide of the poet Gallus) and these examples had, in turn been a re-elaboration of the story of Polyphemus of Theocritus (Idyll XI). By using the same words, the themes are brought back, re-enacted anew in a literary game of recognition and insiders' pleasure.

This weaving of contextual and intertextual conventions works not just as artistic manipulation of language, but importantly as a function of a thematic evocation that is necessary for the contextual *vraisemblance* of the stories. All these stories are, mainly, re-enactments of the past and they are told in the language of past experiences. In these episodic retellings, there is an obvious manipulation of the past as if past episodes were chess figures. This creates an illusion of reality made with the discourse (a pseudo-reality) which in turn underscores the power of art to make us feel, see, and experience what is not there.

Pastoral literary time, as Herbert Lindenberger eloquently argues in his article "The Idyllic Moment," is a special kind of experience ". . . which gains its meaning and intensity through the tensions it creates with the historical world" (25). That is, instead of a chronological continuum, time is a discontinuous series of segments that can be "revisited" by imagination and by art. In these islands of time or *tempus amoenus*, the emotions can be examined and the soul can be restored. But these privileged moments, as creations of the imagination, are precarious because they are constantly in tension with the empirical world. By the use of the cliché themes and the "borrowed" expressions, pastoral poets were enabled to fashion fictional realities that could be brought back again and again as models and prototypes of a different kind of experience: a perfect one.

Their treatment of time, used purposefully as a convention, is an obvious effort to provide a new and different dimension to reality. This has an almost experimental quality. Interestingly, the same authors of the works I have selected demonstrated in their other works (Cervantes, for example, in *Don Quixote*) a clear interest in the technological developments of their age with regard to measuring and studying chronological time and all their technical applications. All of them were in fact involved in one way or another with extra-literary technological activities. Montemayor was a musician and organist at the time of the construction and installation of the famous organs in the Spanish royal chapels. Ronsard had been in charge of the planning and construction of royal monuments at the court of the Valois. As active soldiers, both Cervantes and d'Urfé had been trained in military technology.

---

(25) Herbert Lindenberger, "The Idyllic Moment: On Pastoral and Romanticism" in *College English* 34, no. 3, December 1972, p. 338.

As the artistic manipulation of pastoral time—Golden Age, or Golden Moment—offers a paragon, a model where the conflicts and problems of life can be meaningfully analyzed and considered (though not necessarily solved), the dimension of space is represented in pastoral through the conventionalized symbol of the *locus amoenus*. The myth of the *locus amoenus*, the pleasance, as an artistic representation of nature is one of the many strategies—perhaps the most effective one—to explain the relationship of man to nature. As E. R. Curtius demonstrates in his study of the *topos* (26), this artistic representation of nature is also one of the oldest in Western literature (27). This durability is one more demonstration that eternal relationships can be superbly represented by means of symbols. In these imagined creations—the Golden Age, the *locus amoenus*, the Fountain of True Love—the implications of living in an empirical, changeable world are projected in a totally different light.

The *locus amoenus*, as it is fashioned in our literature, appeared in the Renaissance works in two major forms: the theological paradise (a promise of an everlasting Eden) and

---

(26) "Arcadia was forever being rediscovered. This was possible because the stock of pastoral motifs was bound to no genre and to no poetic form. It found its way in the Greek romance and from there into the Renaissance. From the Romance (Longus), pastoral poetry could return to the Eclogue or pass to the drama (*Pastor Fido*). The pastoral would be as extensive as the knightly world. In the medieval *pastourelle* the two worlds meet. Yes, in the pastoral world all worlds 'embrace one another'." E. R. Curtius, *European Literature and the Latin Middle Ages*, W. R. Trask, translator, Princeton, Princeton University Press, 1953, p. 187.

(27) The pastoral perfect place is very different from non-Western ideas of Paradise. The *locus amoenus* is not the kind of romantic illusion Carlos Castañeda's shaman describes, for instance. The pastoral models follow what Europeans still consider a "natural" environment with all the subsequent implications.

the literary garden. This is what A. Bartlett Giamatti defines as the "Earthly Paradise (28) and what I will now take up.

Arcadia, the pastoral version of the *locus amoenus* symbol is among the most powerful of these earthly paradises. Arcadia includes not only the enchanted place, reflection perhaps of the lost Paradise, but also a physical, possibly real attainable place endowed with all attributes of perfection. As pastoral works attest, this earthly paradise can also be constructed and revisited by rhetorical manipulations of conventions, by the power of the word. The many implications of the symbol can be and have been taken in religious, political, social (29), and political directions but these extend beyond the range of this study. Whatever the applications of the symbol, the *locus amoenus* is one of the oldest and most versatile of conventions, and for pastoral poetics, one of the most important.

In this literature the recurrence of the myth (or symbol) gains further effectiveness precisely because it has been re-enacted by many authors of the genre and thus is available to be adapted and made meaningful again. This is particularly obvious when the circumstances of alienation, self-definition or self-search demand the elaboration of a paragon used as a support or even a contrast.

Employed to contrast the passions (the changes in the lives of humans) with the models of perfection found in nature—i.e. fluidity versus immutability—these earthly paradises are mirrors where suffering humans can find consolation and even cures. That is, they contain a moral lesson taught by contrast. This is the point of the words of Céladon when he addresses the river at Lignon:

---

(28) A. Bartlett Giamatti, *The Earthly Paradise and the Renaissance Epic*, Princeton, Princeton University Press, 1966.

(29) See Raymond Williams, *op. cit.*, and Renato Poggioli, *op. cit.*

Rivière que j'accrois, couché parmi ces fleurs.
Je considère en toi ma triste resemblance;
De deux source tu prends en même temps naissance
et mes yeux ne sont rien que deux sources de pleurs.
Tu n'as point tant de flots que je sens de malheurs:
Si tu cours sans dessein, je sers sans espérance;
En des sommets hautains ta source se commence:
D'orgueilleuse beaute procèdent mes douleurs. (30)

The river of Lignon is here a meaningful, orderly contrast to the turmoil of the shepherds' emotions. Nature in these uses of the convention is represented as a privileged space where the characters can find solitude and distance, the refuge necessary for self-analysis and contemplation.

The contrast between Céladon and this corner of nature is conveyed to the audience by way of a poetic arrangement of the discourse which allows the shepherd to exteriorize and communicate the paradoxical typically pastoral way of dealing with the most personal and most difficult feelings. Through rhetorical means, the most secret feelings can be exteriorized.

The literariness of the Lignon is a leit-motiv in *L'Astrée*, as is the natural milieu of the Ezla River in *La Diana*, the woods of *Arcadia*, and the forest and meadows of the Henares River in *La Galatea*. This literariness is the product of the manipulation of diverse rhetorical and stylistic resources. The *locus amoenus* as a symbol gains its effectiveness precisely because it is repeated in similar ways and circumstances as a convention.

When the readers of *L'Astrée*, for instance, encounter the melancholic Silvandre, going through the solitary woods, a number of familiar *déja vu* features place them in the recognizable *locus* of pastoral:

_____

(30) Quoted from Léon Levrault, *Le Genre pastoral: Son èvolution*, Paris, Editions Paul Delaplane, 1914, pp. 97-98.

Silvandre, épris de Diane, erre la nuit dans un bois. Il va surpendre sans les reconnaître, une conversation de métaphysique amoureuse entre Adamas et Céladon.

La lune alors, comme ci c'eût été pour le convier à demeurer davantage en ce lieu, sembla s'allumer d'une nouvelle clarté. . . . Et . . . Il résolut de passer en ce lieu une partie de la nuit, suivant sa coutume. Car bien souvent se retirant de toute compagnie, pour le plaisir qu'il avait d'entretenir ses nouvelles pensées . . . (31)

Followers of the genre (d'Urfé was among them), can associate Silvandre's promenade with many similar situations of other pastorals. In *La Galatea*, for instance, the narrator places Elicio in the following nocturnal woods:

[Elicio] se entró por la espesura de un espeso bosque adelante, buscando algun solitario lugar . . . por ser cosa ya averiguada que a los tristes imaginativos corazones ninguna cosa les es mayor gusto que la soledad, despertadora de memorias tristes o alegres. (32)

In addition to the similarities between the nocturnal moment and the sentiments of the characters seeking isolation to wander and meditate, there is a literariness expressed by the alliterative use of the *s* sound by both Cervantes and d'Urfé, an intentional play on the alliterative *s* which is associated with silencing someone.

And their choice of poetic means connects these works and other successful novels with the classical masterpieces, models of the pastoral genre. The success of the *locus amoenus* convention is thus based not only on the reproduction of the theme, but also on the display of the rhetorical devices

---

(31) Honoré d'Urfé, *L'Astrée*, Genette edition, p. 137.
(32) Miguel de Cervantes, *La Galatea*, Avalle-Arce edition, Libro Primero, p. 30.

which can lead to the recognition and identification of the convention as such. The pastoral *locus amoenus* then serves not only to contrast with the confusion of the shepherds' feelings, but also acts as a background, a guide, a paragon— i.e. as a symbol.

All of these melancholic and poetic shepherds are found in the midst of a natural environment that has been stylized— captured or tamed—by linguistic categorization and classifications. As the islands of time or idyllic moments, these pastoral *loci* are fragile by contrast with natural reality, but they also have qualities of durability as well. Their durability or tenacity originated both because they have been "re-created" as cliché-like paragons and because they can be recalled by the power of the word. When Carino, mentioned in Prosa 8, revisits with the aid of his memory the pleasant fields where he and his beloved gathered the bountiful fruits, he is reproducing a dream-like corner of reality where everything is perfect and where happiness can be found. It is, in other words, a literary place.

Nature is, in these instances—echoes of the Virgilian shepherds and the Theocritan Cyclops—an orderly, pleasant background where the characters can find solitude and, removed from ordinary activities, can contemplate their situation. Solitude becomes, in these stories, a sentimental state, as well as a conventionalized paradigmatic frame from which the characters can remove themselves and exercise self-assessment. Solitude is here one of the strategies for removing oneself from the ordinary activities and for reaching a state of alienation from the ordinary world. Free from these constraints, the shepherds can contemplate, analyze, and ironically, enjoy the sorrows and contradictions of their situation, as the mentioned narrator explained. "For, as everybody knows, nothing is sweeter than solitude to the sorrowful, imaginative souls for it awakens equally sad and joyful memories."

If this is best realized in the solitude of Nature, nature is then a supposedly organized entity and therefore understood or at least understandable. But this has been the aim of all discourses, dialogues, songs, and descriptions in these pastorals. By verbal, artistic means the organization of the physical environment (classifying, categorizing it), the explanations of their feelings (composing stories), have been carried forward in an effort to grasp and understand that which is complicated and confused.

As in the case of Love, Time, and Fortune, the physical space—man's place in nature—cannot be analyzed as it actually is; that is, in constant movement. In order to bring analysis to the passions, scrutiny to thoughts, these elements have to be isolated and suspended as themes. The difficulties involved in this are obvious and yet pastoral provides a way in which, by verbal cliché, those elements are framed. The feelings are framed not only by verbalization, but by being considered from the perspective of distance, nostalgia, and melancholy.

Melancholy

Why the melancholic twist? Just as in modern literature the perspective for the analysis of realities is one of alienation —a form of distance—so pastoral brings the ephemeral nature of life, the changes, the turmoil out through a general stance of distance provided by melancholy.

Melancholy, as works such as Burton's *Anatomy of Melancholy* (1621) illustrate, was one of the most general preoccupations of the late sixteenth and early seventeenth centuries— equivalent perhaps to the pervasive power that alienation has had in twentieth century art and life. In the case of the great prose romances I am analyzing—as earlier in the case of the *Idylls* and the *Eclogues*—, the general stance or frame is one of acute melancholy experienced by all the characters in these works.

The poet/shepherds, introduced from the very beginning lines of these works in an exacerbated sentimental state, contemplate their fortunes and misfortunes as conditioned by Time, Fate, and universal Eros (in the form of sentimental love). We saw above the way the audience was introduced to the themes and action in *La Diana:*

Baxaba de las montañas de León el olvidado Sireno a quien Amor, la Fortuna, el tiempo, tratavan de manera que del menor mal que en tan triste vida padecĭa, no se esperaba menos que perdella. (33)

Melancholy—black bile—the cold, dry, thick, and sour humor that acts as a bridle to the other two hot humors (choler and blood) affects all humans either in disposition or by the influence of a habit. According to Burton, the latter i.e.: melancholy as habit, seems to tyrannize those unable to overcome the problems that affect all of us and is a chronic disease. Although difficult, it can be cured by several means. The former type, melancholy, is a disposition that is defined in the following terms:

That transitory melancholy which goes and comes upon every small occasion of sorrow, need, sickness, trouble, fear, grief, passion, or perturbations of the mind . . . and from these melancholic dispositions, no man living is free . . . [for] in this life . . . nothing is so prosperous and pleasant, but it has some bitterness in it, some complaining, some grudging; it is all (bitter-sweet). (34)

---

(33) Jorge de Montemayor, *op. cit.*, Livro Primero, p. 9.

(34) Robert Burton, *The Anatomy of Melancholy. What it is, with all the kinds, cures, symptomes, prognostickes & Several cures of it,* Holbrook Jackson, editor, New York, Vintage Books, 1977, pp. 143-144.

Melancholy, in all forms, clouds the mind and confuses the patient, deceiving him/her in the same way that passions deceive the lover or just as fiction, art can deceive the audience. The person attacked by melancholy believes in what is not there. It is in the sense of both cause and cure that melancholy is addressed as the object of countless songs, discussions, and compositions of the pastoral discourse.

For an extensively elaborated example of this type of melancholy we can turn to a passage of L'Astrée

> *Mais il est temps de revenir à Céladon que nous avons si longuement laissé dans se caverne, sans autre compagnie que celle des ses pensées qui n'avient autre sujet que son bonheur passé et son ennui présent.*
>
> *Quinze ou sieze jours s'écoulèrent de cette sorte avec si peu de souci de la vie, que la tristesse le nourrissait plus qu'autre chose qu'il se souciât de manger. Tout son plaisir était en ses imaginations, avec lesquelles il passait les jours et les nuits, qui lui étaient même chose puisqu'éloigné des yeux d'Astrée, les uns et les autres ne lui semblaient que des ténèbres.* (35)

As a result of their frustration, passions and unrelenting grief, Ergasto, Sireno, and, in the above example Céladon—the suffering lovers—are affected by melancholy and have fallen victim to a transitory state of acute sorrow and confusion.

What kind of solutions are offered and discussed in these pastoral works? What is the possible cure among the various remedies known? It is perhaps best seen in *Arcadia* where the whole range (including magical) of remedies is discussed in an organized chapter. Enumerated systematically throughout the Prosas and the complementary Eglogas which echo the ideas expressed in those Prosas, we find many of the various remedies later included by Burton in the Glossary of his cures

---

(35) d'Urfé, *op. cit.*, Genette ed., p. 137.

(36). In more or less explicit ways, we encounter the practices of "confessions to a friend, mirth and merry company, music of all sorts applied . . . counsel, comfort, good persuasion, witty devices, fictions . . . and all kinds of consolations for all discontents and passions of the mind" (37).

But there are also references to other cures which were openly controversial and in direct conflict with the doctrines of the Church. Magical remedies for these maladies appear more or less explicitly as a theme in all pastorals (Montemayor's *Diana* being the most obvious in this regard). Thus we read that, as a group of shepherds sets out to visit the temple of Pan, one—Clonico—decides to take leave of the rest because, as the narrator explains: "He wanted to go finish the business that has been prevented by us the previous evening: that is, to find out a remedy for his troubles through the help of a well-known old wisewoman, a most knowledgable *instructor in magic practices*" (38). But neither the magic of this woman, nor the supernatural powers—over earth, heaven, the sea, the unwearying sun, "incantations," "divinations," etc.—that the old shepherd Enareto of the same Prosa 8 seems to possess are further discussed.

The problem of melancholy is a problem of imbalance (lack of *decorum* and discretion) which affects all melancholic shepherds. The fact is that Clonico, the unfortunate shepherd (*misero pastore*), is ". . . in love beyond the proper limits, and not knowing how to get the governance of himself, is wasted away as utterly as soft wax in fire" (39).

The remedy to this state of being "wasted away," and being melancholic to the extreme, is not given in the form of magic cures. Instead, the cure is provided through the coop-

---

(36) Burton, *op. cit.*, The Second Partition: The Cure of Melancholy, First Section, p. 5.

(37) *Ibid.*, Second Partition, Synopsis 6, pp. 1-4.

(38) Sanazzaro, *Nash translation, op. cit.*, p. 91.

(39) *Ibid.*, p. 94.

eration of all the shepherd/poets and friends in the form of advice, company, music, and the endless reporting of stories and tales which being told in the most hyperbolic terms, serve as models and paragons for the lovelorn shepherd to follow. The troubles of the suffering shepherds are treated, not with empirical products and medicines, but with elaborate, organized verbalizations.

Thus, for example, when the narrator Sincero has finished his story with the singing of the sextine—a further step in the literarization of his report—in Eclogue 7, he makes a transition reporting what was said to him by his friend. The optimistic prediction is, in this case, the promise of a "cure" for the melancholic shepherd and the friend's (Carino) own story is the paradigm for it.

As representative of the cure-model, Carino's incomplete tale is not the total secret of the cure. The structural content of all these narratives requires an accumulation of similar— and at times mirrored—cases from which the lesson can be derived. The point is not to give *one* version of the model-story, but to give as many variations and similarities as can be managed in any given work. That is the reason why all stories and tales of the paradigmatic shepherds succeed one another without reaching definite conclusions or resolutions—although this too may be an indicator of the unpredictability and mystery of the feelings of love.

In the same *Arcadia*, for instance, the story of the episode relating Clonico's "love beyond proper limits" is left in suspended realization by the appearance of yet another equally sorrowful and melancholic shepherd who represents a slightly different version of the problem of love. In his case, the variation is further marked by the initial reluctance of the character to share his tale. His reticence is ironic, for he would expand on it in the following lines. But it serves to stress the intensity of his melancholy and to emphasize his *expressive* skills (40).

The similarity of this Egloga to Theocritus' singing matches in Idylls—"The Herdsmen" (Idyll 4) and "The Goatherd versus the Shepherd" (Idyll 5) and with Virgil's Eclogue 3 has been often pointed to as clear cases of imitation (Nash, 1970: 96, footnote 1). Here it is important to reiterate that these seemingly odd jesting matches interjected in the middle of more serious and loftier discussions remind the audience of several points relevant to the *vraisemblance* of these works (as do the criticisms of the casuistic of Love in *L'Astrée* Premicre Partie Scene between Hylas and Astrée). These discrepancies are important.

In the first place, they are one of the many ways to help cure the melancholy of the affected shepherds. The cure not only comes by way of elevated discourses, but by showing their command of poetic skills and language with exercises of quick answers and ready wit. As such these follow the cure proposed by Burton under the rubric of "witty devices." Secondly, singing contests, judged by the experts of the genre (i.e. Montano in the case above) are not simply exercises of imitation but are required conventions which the followers and students of the works would identify, enjoy, judge—indeed becoming the extrinsic judges of the songs. Thus it is not accidental or merely imitative that examples of this type of singing match are found, not only in Sanazzaro, after Virgil and Theocritus, but also in *La Diana* (Libro Cuarto) and in *La Galatea* (Libro Tercero, "Egloga entre los cuatro discretos y lastimados pastores, Orompo, Marsilio, Crisio y Orfenio"). They are there in function of a total view.

Pastoral literature, thus, using these different approaches —witty, lofty, euphonic—represents a cure for melancholy.

---

(40) Cf. Sanazzaro's *Arcadia*, Portirelli edition, Egloga 9, pp. 118 and 122.

The cure of literary art, with its emphasis on special language and a selection of themes, constitutes an argument which the cultivators of this art obviously found convincing. If melancholy is a special state, a condition that is other-than-the-ordinary state, pastoral literature, exploiting as it does the powers of artistic illusion (that which is other-than-the-ordinary), is a most appropriate treatment.

Authors and audiences of pastoral are always aware that they are seeking and cultivating fiction, but with a purpose. In the fictional model, all those involved find the means to make sense out of the experiences beyond the individual's normal control. In this sense, the paradigmatic stories are also a kind of solution, a cure for the effects of disorderly events, troublesome passions which are so difficult otherwise to explain and understand. Finally, the apparent discrepancies between the serious, sorrowful discourses of the lovesick shepherds and these lighthumored and witty repartees point out once more the gamelike quality that these pastoral verbal exercises entail. This is a game which, in addition to linking the audiences to a wider intertextual field, provides a form of distantiation that makes empirical events understandable in a new perspective.

In conclusion, the authors of pastoral were perfectly aware that to deal with frustrations, the problems and feelings of being in a depressed state, the artist—as maker of realities other than empirical ones—has several different choices. One is to expose the experiences and the conditions surrounding human affairs in all their crude detail and "realism." A second is to attack these conditions by distorting artistically the persons and/or institutions responsible or deemed responsible for the state of unfairness. A third choice is to explain those situations by defining the experiences through euphemic or euphonic terms. This third choice is the avenue or vehicle chosen by the cultivators of pastoral art.

Empson says, "Dramatizing the literary metaphor, the power of beauty is like the power of magic; both are individualist, dangerous, and outside the social order, but it is so strong that it brings out other ideas which were at the back of the metaphor (41).

It is undeniable that those different choices and any other artistic mechanisms have in common the double polarity between the thing represented and the representation itself. This, in fact, is a mechanism exploited by all forms of symbolic systems, a point made well by Geertz:

The drive to make sense out of experience, to give it form and order, is evidently as real and as pressing as the more familiar biological needs. And this being so, it seems unnecessary to continue to interpret symbolic activities—religion, art, ideology—as nothing but thinly disguised expressions of something other than what they seem to be: attempts to provide orientations for an organism which cannot live in a world that it is unable to understand. If symbols, to adapt a phrase of Kenneth Burke's, are strategies for encompassing situations, then we need to give more attention to how people define situations and how they go about coming to terms with them. (42)

The pastoral chooses as a medium the composition of fictional worlds that magnify the positive and refined as an aesthetic solution or cure. The three main thematic frames cultivated in pastoral involve either taking refuge in a different-from-the-present, more orderly time (the Golden Age), by seeking a categorical, perfect place or environment (the *locus amoenus*), or by devising a differently arranged society (the world of the sophisticated, aristocratic, albeit melancholy shepherd).

---

(41) William Empson, *op. cit.*, p. 33.
(42) Clifford Geertz, "Ethos, World-View, and the Analysis of Sacred Symbols," in C. Geertz, *The Interpretation of Cultures*, New York, Basic Books, 1973, pp. 140-141.

Since the earliest literary documents, reality has been depicted either as something perfect or perfectible—in a constant state of betterment or else as a fallen paradise. The themes of sadness and melancholy that frame and condition the pastoral stories are directly derived from the latter view: the contemplation of disorder, conflict, and turmoil.

And yet in this enterprise—as in any other artistic one—there is a clear element of play as well. There is a playfulness in the stories, a sort of positive moral. Messages can be extracted, lessons can be learned from the emulation of the productions of the past. And the authors and their audiences know that these situations are not empirical ones, that these worlds are in some sense false. This very contradiction is part and parcel of the aesthetics of the pastoral genre. This is where the *fingere*, the efforts of fictionality and art gain import.

CHAPTER VI

INNOVATION AND TYPICALITY IN PASTORAL POETICS: THE CASE OF *LA GALATEA*

As a consequence of the particular aesthetic demands of the genre, pastoral romances of the Renaissance raise a number of issues that extend beyond the genre itself. Since pastoral poetics are based on purposeful recuperation of earlier texts through the repetition, quotation, and reproduction of themes and expressions already used in other works, the analyst is confronted with specific problems of literary production and literary interpretation. The very emphasis that pastoral places on conventions of recuperation raises the question of the uniqueness of works and the characteristics that make them belong to a genre. It also poses the dilemma of distinguishing between original, major authors and secondary, slavish followers of rules. How it is possible to produce a unique work when the rules emphasize the continual reproduction of lexical, rhetorical, and thematic conventions and how works are produced that both reinforce conventions and subvert them without losing the necessary overall identification with the genre are the central questions here. The analytical task is to look for those individual characteristics that, serving to re-enact the conventions, mark any particular work with an identity of its own.

Because of the complexities and subtleties involved, the questions of continuity and innovation can only be addressed through the analysis of a particular work in which these and related issues can be directly examined. Among the many possible choices, I have selected *La Galatea* by Cervantes for this purpose, both because of my personal interest in Cervantes' work and because it is a work that well represents these issues. It is representative both in the sense of clarifying the characteristics that mark a work as belonging to the genre of pastoral, and in providing a review of the questions relevant to uniqueness and originality.

Published in 1585, after the fame of Sanazzaro's *Arcadia* (1504) (1) and Montemayor's *Diana* (1559) was well established and when the popularity of the pastoral romances was at its peak, this first fictional narrative by Cervantes was itself subjected to imitation and even plagiarism (2). It has also been at various times the center of debates regarding its own merits—as a seminal work, as a precursor or preparation for Cervantes' masterpiece, or as a cliché-laden exercise in imitation.

Jas. Fitzmaurice-Kelly, in his introduction to *La Galatea* comments: "Cervantes is admittedly a wonderful creator; but the pastoral of his time,—a pastiche or mosaic of conventional figures—gave no opportunity of displaying his powers as an inventor" (3). Juan Bautista Avalle-Arce only admits

---

(1) *Arcadia* was first translated into Spanish in Toledo in 1549 with great popular success. See Rafael Ferreres, "Prólogo" to *La Diana enamorada* by Gil Polo, Madrid, Clásicos castellanos, Espasa-Calpe, 1962, p. xii.

(2) Cf. Juan Bautista Avalle-Arce. *La novela pastoril española*, Madrid, Istmo, 1974, especially Chapter IV; "Las continuaciones de La Diana," pp. 101-139, and Chapter VII; "Los italianizantes," pp. 203-207.

(3) Jas. Fitzmaurice-Kelly, "Introduction," *The Complete Works of Miguel de Cervantes; La Galatea*, vol. XII, H. Oelsner and A. B. Welford transl., Glasgow, Gowans and Gray, 1903, p. xxxiv.

the existence of a connection between *La Galatea* and Spanish pastorals. Although he recognizes a few points of formal similarity between *La Galatea* and Sanazzaro's *Arcadia*, he dismisses any ties linking these two pastoral works. Avalle-Arce argues "El último punto a tratar se refiere a la posible influencia de Sannazaro. Desde un punto de vista formal no hay parecido alguno, ya que como queda indicado, Cervantes parte de los modelos españles del género. . . . De todas maneras, se puede afirmar que nada de importancia en la *Galatea* deriva de la novela italiana" (4).

Against this opinion, Mia Gerhardt sees *La Galatea* as a work based on the conventions of the genre including those elaborated by Sanazzaro. In her opinion, this does not diminish its merits. Gerhardt says:

> *Tout autre [que G. de Montalvo] est le cas de Cervantes qui en 1585 débute dans la carrière des lettres avec sa* **Galatea.** *On a coutume d'en dire beaucoup de mal, probablement par comparison avec les chefs-d'oeuvre de l'auteur, car en elle-même la* **Galatea** *n'est pas inférieure à bien d'autres romans pastoreaux. . . . L'originalité de l'élément pastoral est dans le fait même qu'il est étroitement imité de Sanazaro; les discussions philosophiques sur l'amour sont inspirées de Léon Hebreo, le "Chant de Calliope" est une transposition dans le domain littéraire des intermèdes patriotiques de ses prédécesseurs.* (5)

Accepting a wide range of possibilities for the pastoral background of *La Galatea*, Francisco López Estrada comments:

---

(4) Juan Bautista Avalle-Arce, *op. cit.*, p. 248.
(5) Mia Irene Gerhardt, *op. cit.*, p. 191.

La tradición española ofrecía a Cervantes un mosaico de influencias clásicas adonde podía acudir para escoger aquellas que creyera más adecuadas a sus fines. La Arcadia de Sannazaro, es la obra típica y la que presenta en este aspecto una más extensa suma de influencias; añádase a la Arcadia la novelística pastoril hispánica; y tambien la intricada red, tejida por la lírica pastoril en torno a los temas clásicos, y aún más, recogiendo el eco italiano de estos temas. (6)

The common denominator of these various remarks is an interest in tracing the links between the different themes and rhetorical forms in *La Galatea* to the sources from which Cervantes could and probably did borrow major elements. There is also an implicit and explicit intent to produce a norm of excellence by which the work can be measured (7). In most cases this measure is another major work of the genre (Montemayor's *Diana*), in many others it is Cervantes' own later work. And there are other normative judgments that affect the reading of *La Galatea* in ways unrelated to its particular merits as a text (8).

The studies of these prestigious Cervantists rightly point to Cervantes' use of the conventions of pastoral as his particular

---

(6) Francisco López Estrada, *op. cit.*, p. 53.

(7) *Ibid.*, p. 65.

(8) Avalle-Arce says: "Hay demasiada literatura para que ésto pueda ser vida, y un exceso de vida que la aleja del idealismo del género. Esta respuesta ha fallado, pero ya habrá otras a cuya intelección recta ayudará la lectura de su primera novela. Avalle-Arce, *op. cit.*, p. 247.

Gerald Brenan says: "It was natural for Cervantes, a person in love, to have started his literary career with a pastoral. Although *La Galatea* is unreadable, we can appreciate it as part of Cervantes training for other works," in "Cervantes," *Asomante*, VII (1951), p. 20.

Agustin G. de Amézua y Mayo also thinks that *La Galatea* was written as preparation for other works. He gives special attention to the episodes of Lisandro and Leonida and that of "Los dos amigos." *Cervantes, creador de la novela corta española*, Madrid, CSIC, 1956-1958, vol. 2.

voluntad de estilo (López Estrada, 1948:53) or as the consistent features that become part of Cervantes' recognizable artistry (Avalle-Arce, 1974:229-263). Despite the merit and interest of these approaches, there are aspects of the actual processes of concretization of the work and of authorial purposes which the search for sources, influences, and norms of comparison does not satisfactorily answer. It is to those aspects of the artistic task, specifically to the process of interpretation and composition implied in a creative work, that I turn in the analysis of *La Galatea.*

La Galatea: Structure and Themes

To begin, a description of the actual structure of the book is needed, in order to examine the way Cervantes integrated the linguistic and rhetorical devices of the genre with his chosen themes. A close study of some of the most consistent patterns of this integration in *La Galatea* provides a way to understand how Cervantes approaches the general literary conventions of his day as well as his personal experiments in literature, his version of *decorum* (9), and his innovations within the pastoral genre. A brief analysis of the "Canto de Calíope," in itself a convention following a long series of laudatory *cantos* in pastoral (10), will follow to clarify the meaning of its insertion within the structure of *La Galatea.*

---

(9) As explained in his "Prólogo to the Curious readers," and later in Libro Sexto, Cervantes' idea of *decorum*, includes the principles of unity and harmony of the composition implied in the general sense of the concept. But in his interpretation there is a confluence of art, industry (dedication), and talent—a praxis—that changes the artistic effort into a "third nature." (See page 160 and the discussion of the "Canto de Calíope" below.)

(10) Many critics, such as Fitzmaurice-Kelly, López Estrada, and Avalle-Arce among others, agree to consider the "Canto del Turia" by Gil Polo, as the immediate predecessor of the "Canto de Calíope."

Although the structure of *La Galatea* follows the pattern established at least since *La Diana*, it presents interesting characteristics which are worthy of analysis. But the critics have largely relegated analysis of the structure to the level of a secondary consideration. This is probably because of the interest and durability that the themes and expressions introduced or adapted by Cervantes have in his artistic production as a whole and because of the influence that those themes and literary inventions have had on the literature of Spain and indeed, of the world. Without denying their importance, I argue here that both the stories and the language —rhetorical devices adapted from the epic, "borrowed verses," pastoral multifaceted names, as well as the elaboration of themes—can be better appreciated if examined within the total structural framework of *La Galatea*.

The action of *La Galatea* begins with a series of *octavas reales* (11) where the pastoral themes of unrequited love, melancholy, and misfortune are announced. The book itself begins with a prologue addressed by the author "To the Curious readers" and three sonnets dedicated by poets, contemporaries of Cervantes, to the author and to the book. Of the *libros* announced as the total work, only six were written. Because then, *La Galatea*, like the majority of Spanish pastorals, is an incomplete work, some of the themes, particularly the story of the shepherdess Galata herself, do not have a resolution nor can we know the actual completion of the plot. While this fact adds interest and even a certain coherence to *La Galatea*, its implications are the source of speculations that extend beyond the scope of this study.

Avalle-Arce however, rightly places this laudatory expression within a long Spanish tradition going back to San Isidoro's *Laudes Hispaniae*. Cf. Avalle-Arce, *op. cit.*, p. 118. There are even older sources; i.e. Aristotle's *Poetics*. See the discussion of the "Canto" below.

(11) After *La Galatea*, many other pastorals adopted the *octava real* for their beginnings. One such example is *El Pastor de Iberia* by Bernardo de la Vega (1591). Cf. Avalle-Arce, *op. cit.*, p. 157.

In common with the pastorals of the Renaissance and their antecedents and derivations, the themes of love, fortune, and time set against a "natural" conventional background, are developed throughout the six *libros* or partitions of *La Galatea*. Underlying those themes and their many secondary derivations, there is a recurrent theme often neglected by the critics: the depiction of literature itself. This theme appears constantly, although not explicitly in all cases. Consistent with the approach taken in *La Galatea* to other themes, literary art itself is presented as an enumeration of the multiple roles of words (Libro Quinto), as quotations of other texts, disguised as music, and even as the allegorical figure of a Muse (Calliope). On a few occasions, such as in the "Canto a Calíope" and Telesio's discourse in Book Six, the theme of literary art is openly discussed and literature is praised as the central aim of pastoral discourse. This point lies at the center of my analysis.

Literature as a Theme

The concern with literature, with poetics in a general sense, is directly addressed in the very first words of the opening Prólogo of *La Galatea* and becomes one of its leitmotifs.

Curiosos lectores:

La ocupación de escrebir [sic] *églogas en tiempo que, en general, la poesía anda tan desfavorecida, bien recelo que no será tenido por ejercicio tan loable que no sea necesario dar alguna particular satisfacción. . . . Más, pues a ninguno toca satisfacer a ingenios que se encierran en términos tan limitados sólo quiero responder a los que, libres de pasión, con mayor fundamento se mueven a no admitir las diferencias de la poesía vulgar. . . . De más que de que no puede negarse que los estudios desta facultad—en el pasado tiempo, con razón, tan estimada—traen consigo más que medianos provechos, como son enriquecer el poeta considerando su propia lengua, y enseñorearse del artificio de la elocuencia que en ella cabe, para empresas más altas y de mayor importancia, abrir camino para que, a su imitación, los ánimos estrechos, que en la brevedad del lenguage antiguo quieren que se acabe la abundancia de la lengua castellana, entiendan que tienen campo abierto, fértil y espacioso por el cual, con facilidad y dulzura, con gravedad y elocuencia, pueden correr con libertad, descubriendo la diversidad de conceptos agudos, graves, sotiles y levantados que en la fertilidad de los ingenios españoles la favorable influencia del cielo con tal ventaja en diversas partes ha producido y cada hora produce en la edad dichosa nuestra.* (12)

A number of studies have assessed the possible meanings, authorial attitude, and implications of this Prologue (13). Even if the words of the Prologue remind us to take into consideration Cervantes' own artistic irony (14), we must also

---

(12) Miguel de Cervantes Saavedra, *La Galatea*, Juan Bautista Avalle-Arce, editor, Madrid, Clásicos castellanos, Espasa-Calpe, 1968, pp. 5-7.

(13) All commentators of *La Galatea* have written on the matter. A good discussion is provided by E. C. Riley in his *Cervantes's Theory of the Novel*, Oxford, Oxford U. Press, 1968, pp. 86-94. A criticism of another kind qualifies Cervantes' attitude toward pastoral as ambivalent and even hypocritical, since in spite of the words of the "Prólogo," he seems to attack the genre in other works (i.e. *El coloquio de los perros* where Berganza refers to pastorals as "Cosas soñadas y bien escritas para entretenimiento de los ociosos y no verdad alguna"). Cf. Rafael Ferreres, *op. cit.*, p. xxiv.

(14) I am using the term here according to the definition given by Northrop Frye, *Anatomy of Criticism: Four Essays*, cited ed., pp. 40-41. See also Chapter IV of this book. William Empson expands on the tension that exists between what is said and what is shown. Cf. W. Empson, *Some Versions of Pastoral*, Norfolk, New Directions Books, 1950, pp. 55-56.

search for the other leads which this introductory declaration contains and then find in the text as a whole the consistencies between those initial leads and the possible confirmation and repetition of those elements in words, characters, rhetorical devices, and themes.

From these very introductory lines, a self-analytical reflection on the subject of writing poetry, and more specifically pastoral poetry begins: ". . . the occupation of writing eglogues, at a time when poetry is generally regarded with such little favor." It serves to spell out the purpose of poetry, the role of the poet, and the state of the art: ". . . It cannot be denied that studies in this art—in former times so highly esteemed and rightly so—carry with them no inconsiderable advantages."

Cervantes' recurrent concern with poetry is part of his general concern with the power of art. This is expressed by Telesio in the Libro Sexto:

Y la industria de sus moradores ha hecho tanto, que la naturaleza, encorporada con el arte, es hecha artífice y connatural del arte, y de entrambas a dos se ha hecho una tercia naturaleza, a la cual no sabré dar nombre. (15)

Industry (effort and praxis) plus natural talent added to artifice bring forward a third nature which draws equally from nature and from art. On this I shall comment below.

Interest in language and the power of linguistic art was a general concern of the time expressed in the numerous works on language, diction, and style (16). Cervantes himself never

---

(15) Miguel de Cervantes, *op. cit.*, Libro Sexto, p. 170.

(16) Among the best known are Juan de Valdés' *Diálogo de la lengua*, Alcalá, 1529, and Alfonso Sánchez de Lima's, *El arte poética en romance castellano*, Alcalá, 1580. Valdés lived in Naples for a few years and enjoyed there a good reputation among the humanists. His book was not published in Spain for some time because of his "Erasmista" ideology.

abandoned his interest in art, poetry, and literature and, years after the publication of *Galatea*, he repeats similar lines about art in *Don Quixote:*

> . . . *La poesía, señor hidalgo, a mi parecer, es como una doncella tierna y de poca edad, y en todo estremo hermosa, a quien tienen cuidado de enriquecer, pulir y adornar otras muchas doncellas, que son todas las otras ciencias.* (17).

Spelling out the "considerable advantages" that the exercise of the cultivation of pastoral poetry affords, the self-analysis expounded in the Prologue turns into an open invitation for other poets and for the reader to join in the renewal effort which will bring enrichment and expansion to their native tongue.

Cervantes' invitation, as the heading indicates, is addressed to a special kind of reader, not the *vulgo*, but the motivated, interested, and skilled "curious readers" (18). While it is possible that the audience would be mostly composed of fellow writers, it is in their capacity as readers and collaborators that they will be able to participate in the task of construction, through renewal, of art. It is also in this capacity that we, at a distance of four hundred years, are able to follow and interpret the leads offered by the text.

The cultivation of the eclogues—pastoral art—says the prologue, offers "an open, easy, spacious field" where we can find the polyfaceted value of poetry. This polyfaceted dimension of poetry and of art is one of the most consistent ideas developed in *La Galatea*. It appears in the actual use of language; in the structure of the episodes; in the disposition and interventions of the characters; and in themes, images and

---

(17) Miguel de Cervantes, *Don Quijote*, II, XVI, ed. by Martín de Riquer, Barcelona, Juventud, 1959, p. 649.

(18) Addressing the audience in this way was also a convention of the time.

metaphors. This is summarized as the metaphor of the "fractured mirror" included in the discussion of the theme of love in the first pages of the First Book. Erastro says:

> No se ven tantos rostros figurados
> en roto espejo, o hecho por tal arte,
> que si uno en él se mira, retratados
> se ve una multitud en cada parte. (19)

And the idea of the multiplicity of faces reflected in a "fractured or artistically composed mirror" is continued later in the book.

The talent for combining a variety of possibilities within an organic, coherent body of work is the reason why one of the poets mentioned by Calliope is praised in the following terms:

> Cual suele estar de variadas flores
> adorno y rico el más florido Mayo,
> tal de mil varias ciencias y primores
> está el ingenio de don Juan Aguayo. (20)

Variety worked within an organic unity by a "good intelligence," as Don Quijote's Canon later advises (32), is one of the cornerstones of Cervantes' philosophy of composition in *La Galatea*. It is also one of the macro-contexts, in the sense of an agreement shared by many of the theorists and writers in Cervantes' time (22).

The conventional "Che per tal variar natura è bella" the variety of possibilities is a sentence that Damon, one of the

---

(19) Miguel de Cervantes, *La Galatea*, Avalle-Arce editor, Libro Primero, p. 25.
(20) *Ibid.*, Libro Sexto, p. 209.
(21) *Ibid., Don Quijote*, I, XLVII, Martin de Riquer, ed., p. 351.
(22) E. C. Riley, *op. cit.*, pp. 116-130.

poet/shepherds of *La Galatea*, cites verbatim in his sonnet in Libro Quinto:

La noche al día, y el calor al frío,
la flor al fruto van en seguimiento,
formando de contrarios igual tela.

La sujeción se cambia en señorío,
en placer el pesar, la gloria en viento,
'che per tal variar natura è bella'. (23)

The inclusion of those famous words in a character's poem does not obscure the fact that the singer of this sonnet is also elaborating and repeating the themes of change and fluidity basic to the pastoral genre. The image of the sea as a theater of continuity, variety, and change reflects in turn the main idea elaborated by López Maldonado in his dedicatory sonnet, included at the beginning of the work "Salen del mar, y vuelven a sus senos/ después de una veloz larga carrera."

Thus the three sonnets dedicated to the author by Luis Gálvez de Montalvo, Luis Vargas Manrique, and Gabriel López Maldonado (24) placed between the Prologue and the actual narrative of *La Galatea* may have a function larger than the mere gesture of recognition of praise of Cervantes. This repetition and reappearance of words, authors, and themes is further supported by the inclusion of these same authors in his monument to the variety, richness, and eloquence of the cultivators of Spanish poetry: the *Canto de Calíope*.

Variety, in this sense, is a source of beauty and pleasure which Cervantes translated into a technique, his version of *decorum* which is expressed in his pastoral by reproducing

---

(23) Miguel de Cervantes, *La Galatea*, Avalle-Arce, editor, Libro Quinto, p. 102.

(24) These three poets were greatly admired by Cervantes, Gálvez de Montalvo was also praised by *el cura* and *el ama* in *Don Quijote*, I, XVI.

stories that reflect each other, characters who quote famous words, often uttering sentences that are echoes or actual "découpages" of other sentences, all within the unifying frame of a multivoiced discourse (25). The inclusion of still many other voices from the past (i.e. Garcilaso's and even Virgil's) is an added feature which Cervantes could exploit precisely because the conventions of the genre allowed and even dictated the repetition of earlier works. And yet *La Galatea* remains coherent.

The ability to maintain a cohesive harmony, which we describe with the imprecise term style, is one of the characteristics that mark the difference between *La Galatea* and the merely imitative sequels so abundant in pastoral. To this I shall return below. The idea of a segmented whole, of working artistically with aspects of literature and with aspects of reality to form a unified picture, is a convention which Cervantes adopts in his work as a whole; it is part of his artistic and philosophical *vraisemblance* or *decorum*. It is also one of the most clearly distinguishable leads offered to the reader in this his first artistic narrative. In the lines of the Prologue, we find an open invitation to join in the activity of renewal which will enrich and universalize Cervantes' national literature, and also an invitation to reflect on art in general and particularly on literary art. In its cultivation, the open minded souls can find "a field easy and spacious which they can freely traverse with ease and sweetness . . . discovering the acute, subtle, weighty and elevated thoughts."

Nested Episodes

We can now turn to the analysis of that "spacious, open field" of the text. The structure of *La Galatea* is built accord-

---

(25) E. C. Riley comments on this point: "The idea of organic unity underlies Cervantes' notion of formal literary beauty. It is the standard one inherited from Antiquity and transmitted by Christian writers." *Op. cit.*, p. 118.

ing to a system of episodic alternating prose/verse juxtapositions; a pattern adopted following Sanazzaro's *Arcadia* and later conventionalized by authors of pastoral prose romances, especially after Montemayor's *Diana*.

After the exhortative introduction/prologue and the sonnets of praise, the Libro Primero of *La Galatea* begins with the story of the shepherd Elicio who, together with Erastro will be part of the central narrative throughout the six books. As in other works of the genre, here the reader is acquainted with these characters through the descriptions, settings, and words of the commentator as well as through the characters' own stories, dialogues, and songs.

These lines, already quoted as exemplary of the use of poetic language to depict a pastoral—categorized—nature are a significant choice here for additional reasons. The compositional length and the internal unity of the *octava real* makes these strophes suitable for synthesizing the themes that will be developed later. This reduction/expansion is one of the techniques, although not the only one, that, coming from the opening prologue, underpin the structure of the whole work. The reverse—long story/recapitulation—is also used for narrative effect in the development of the story. In the particular case of the Libro Primero, the opening *octava real* depicts, in emblem-like form, the themes of the hunter (Eros) and the hunted (by *saeta, flecha, lazo, fuego*) which reappear, a few pages later, in an expanded version when the traitor Carino falls victim to the punishing weapons of the vengeful Lisandro.

Thus Elicio, the elegant poet, singing in a typically melancholic tone the themes of love, (mis)fortune, and sorrow, also predicts what for some Renaissance theorists of pastoral (e.g. Herrera) (26) would be inconceivable in pastoral: death and

---

(26) Fernando de Herrera, "Las anotaciones de Herrera," in *Poesía de Boscán y Garcilaso*, Habana, Consejo Nacional de Cultura, 1963, p. 249.

violent acts. But contrary to the Herrerian perception, the presence of death was a pastoral convention ever since the laments for Daphnis in the *Idylls*, Massilia's funeral in Boccaccio's *Ninfale Fiesolano*, and Carino's suicidal threats in Sanazzaro's *Arcadia*. The theme of love as an arrow, a bow, and as fire, found in many examples of lyric poetry, was also used in *La Diana*'s Livro Tercero (27), already quoted. The mixture of melancholic, sentimental, and violent themes is announced in the opening lines of *La Galatea* and is thus perfectly consistent with a convention of the genre. And these themes are consistent as well with the proposed cultivation of variety, which, as the prologue tells us, pastoral poetry affords.

Here we are also given the first clues about how to understand the underlying purpose of Cervantes' art and his philosophy of artistic truth. Making the themes obvious and integrating them in his new version with considerable artistry, Cervantes proves his knowledge of past masters' art. He also shows that the incorporation of established techniques, verses, or themes, when done by an artist, is not an exercise in imitation but an act of *praxis*: artistic, meaningful recuperation. In this and many instances to be seen below, the differences between Cervantes and his imitators comes into clear view. Sequel writers, such as Jerónimo de Tejeda (28), Francisco de Lugo y Dávila (29), Alonso Pérez (30), and others

---

(27) Jorge de Montemayor, *Los siete libros de la Diana*, ed. cited, Livro Tercero, p. 151.

(28) Jerónimo de Tejeda was the author of the sequel *La Diana de Montemayor, Nuevamente compuesto* [sic] *por Hierónimo de Texeda Castellano. Intérprete de lenguas, residente en la villa de Paris, do se da fin a las Historias de la Primera y Segunda Parte* (Paris, 1627).

(29) Francisco de Lugo y Dávila, author of *Teatro Popular* (Madrid, 1622), considers *decorum* as a literal agreement between the characters role and their speech. Thus a shepherd should speak as a shepherd, a courtier according to the language of the court. Cf. Avalle-Arce, *op. cit.*, p. 107.

(30) Alonso Pérez, author of another *Diana* published in Valencia, 1563 and 1564.

were also using the conventional techniques of *amplificatio* —derivations of stories, multiplications of characters, re-enactment of poems and expressions. In their case, however, the technique remains a technique. Unable to maintain coherence between the stories and losing sight of the purpose of quoting poems and sentences from earlier pastorals, their sequels read as collages of quotations, and their themes often seem to be desperate efforts to complete the ambiguous situations left open in the original pastorals they are imitating— marrying the characters off (even when delaying their reunion) or providing other kinds of conclusions to unfinished situations (31).

We can trace instances of Cervantes' integrative processes in the analysis of the language and themes of *La Galatea*. The melancholic song of Elicio, with its disclaimers of humility and clumsiness—"el triste lamentable acento/ del mal acorde son del canto mio"—is followed by several prose paragraphs where the commentator's voice praises the merits and the art of the singer, explains the reasons for Elicio's state, and introduces Galatea, the subject and main character of the book, to the audience:

> *Esto cantaba Elicio, pastor en las riberas del Tajo, con quien naturaleza se mostró tan liberal, cuanto la fortuna y el amor escasos, aunque los discursos del tiempo, consumidor y renovador de las humanas obras, le trujeron a términos que tuvo por dichosos los infinitos y desdichados en que se había visto, y en los que su deseo le había puesto, por la incomparable belleza de la sin par Galatea, pastora en las mismas riberas **nacida** . . . de tan alto y subido entendimento que las **discretas** damas en los reales palacios **crecidas** y al **discreto** tracto de la corte acostumbradas, se*

---

(31) A complete discussion of the passages, poems, and themes lifted literally by Tejeda is found in Avalle-Arce, *La novela pastoril española*, cited ed., pp. 128-136.

*tuvieran por dichosas de parecerla en algo, así en la dis-
creción como en la hermosura.* (32)

In this and throughout the entire book, there is a very
special echo or counter-dialogue between the expressions and
actions carried on by the characters themselves, and the voice
of this omniscient, omnipresent commentator. His voice—re-
capitulating, announcing, or comparing the different ongoing
activities—gives more clear dimension to the songs of the
shepherds or to what the actual development of the episodes
had only hinted at or had left unstressed.

The pattern of song/commentary/ interpolated poems/
prose/dialogues is one of the structural conventions of the
prose pastoral romances, successfully established in pastoral
since Sanazzaro. Cervantes' reproduction of this technique
involves in this and the following passages, an emphasis on
the role of the commentator. To this is added a clear exploi-
tation of the grammatical and rhetorical resources of the
Spanish language (e.g. *el cura, lo cura, locura*) (33), and the
conventional flexibility of pastoral stylistic devices afforded
by the genre itself.

In the previous passage, for instance, a series of hyperboles
("con quien la naturaleza se mostró tan liberal cuanto la fortuna y el amor escasos . . . infinitos y desdichados, . . .")
undercut the disclaimer of clumsiness and lack of art which
Elicio uses to describe his situation and his art. That is to say,

---

(32) Miguel de Cervantes, *La Galatea*, Avalle-Arce, editor, p. 16. Emphasis mine.

(33) "Si no he procurado mil veces quitarla de la memoria, y si otras
tantas no he andado a los médicos y *curas* del lugar a que mediesen
remedio para las ansias que por su causa padezco. Los unos me mandan
que tome no sé qué bebedizos de paciencia; los otros dicen que me en-
comiende a Dios que todo *lo cura*, o que todo es *locura*." This last sentence "o que todo es locura" where the subject predicate ("ellos me
dicen") is omitted, represents a case of grammatical ellipsis exploited
here to keep the phonetic sameness uninterrupted and the repetition of
the sounds thus reinforced. *La Galatea, ibid.*, p. 23.

when the artistic song and the added explanation from both the character and the observer are put together, the reader is given a better picture, though still an incomplete one to which more will be added. Through this, the reader can gradually arrive at a fuller understanding of the questions at hand. Then more facets are added and, in this case, a second character comes to contrast and complement the first.

Once within the frame of Elicio's story (34), through his poems and the commentator's lines, the audience learns of Erastro, a new character who is to become inseparable from the first:

> *No dejara tan presto el agradable canto el enamorado Elicio, si no sonaran a su derecha mano las voces de Estrastro. . . . Venía Erastro acompañado de sus mastines . . . a quién llamaba "León," a quién "Gavilán," a quién "Robusto," a quién "Manchado"; y ellos, como si de entendimiento fueran dotados, viniéndose para él, daban a entender el gusto que de su gusto sentían. . . . Desta manera llegó Erastro adonde de Elicio fue agradablemente recibido.* (35)

Introduced as in a theatrical scene, "a su mano derecha," we encounter here the first pair of parallel-lives (Elicio's and Erastro's) which, together with that of Galatea, form one of the many sentimental triangles in this view of multifaceted love, fickle fortune, and passing time. Audiences that followed pastoral romances, and therefore were knowledgable

---

(34) A second poem, the *coplas reales* "Amoroso pensamiento . . ." sung by Elicio was according to Avalle-Arce, plagiarized by Jerónimo de Tejeda in his mentioned sequel, *La Diana de Montemayor. Nuevamente compuesto.* According to the same critic, they were composed originally, in a somewhat different version by Comendador Escrivá, and later repeated by Cervantes himself in *Don Quijote*, II, XXXVIII. Cf. *La Galatea*, Avalle-Arce, editor, p. 18, footnotes 9 and 16.

(35) Miguel de Cervantes, *La Galatea*, Avalle-Arce, editor, Libro Primero, pp. 20-22.

regarding their conventions, also encounter again the familiar pastoral dogs, here doubled in number and with Spanish names. The dogs bring their proverbial faithfulness and characteristic markings to the pastoral scene. Their presence adds perhaps a touch of humor and their names—Manchado, Robusto, Gavilán, León—echo Melampus (*Idylls*), Melampo (*Arcadia*), Argus (*The Odyssey*), and Adro (*Arcadia*), identifying them with well-known conventional literary animals of earlier pastorals. Here we have a subtle instance in which a seemingly realistic touch points to other literary texts. The audiences recognize the characters and the figures in the landscape not because they are vivid but because they are "recognizable" archetypes.

Contrasting with that pastoral scene, a change in tone and scene then takes place. The commentator records and organizes the background where a very surprising and dramatic scene occurs: Carino's assassination. This murder may have been placed at the beginning of the novel in an attempt to illustrate the extremes of the shepherds' passions. As such this episode would anticipate and contrast with other stories and arguments in the text (e.g. the death of Leonida later in the Book). From a technical point of view, this episode is unusual in a more important way. In contrast to the majority of the stories and vignettes of the book as a whole, this episode is not recounted, remembered by the characters and retold as a thing of the past. The murder "happens" right in front of the shepherds' eyes. While Elicio and Erastro talk, a stranger appears in the scene and is killed by another who was running after him:

Tras él venía otro ligero pastor, que a pocos pasos alcanzó al primero, y asiéndole por el cabezón del pellico, levantó el brazo en el aire cuanto pudo, y un agudo puñal que sin vaina traía se lo encondió dos veces en el cuerpo diciendo:

—Recibe, ¡oh mal lograda Leonida!, la vida deste traidor, que en venganza de tu muerte sacrifico.

*Y ésto fue con tanta presteza hecho, que no tuvieron
lugar Elicio y Erastro de estorbárselo, porque llegaron a
tiempo que ya el herido pastor daba el último aliento,
envuelto en estas pocas y mal formadas palabras:*

*—Dejárasme Lisandro, satisfacer al cielo con más largo
arrepentimiento el agravio que te hice, y después qui-
tárasme la vida, que agora, por la causa que he dicho, mal
contenta destas carnes se aparta.*

*Y sin poder decir más, cerró los ojos en sempiterna
noche.* (36)

The disparity between this scene and the way it is presented, in comparison with the other episodes, creates an
aura of "factuality," of veracity, which contrasts with the
numerous indirectly reported, carefully arranged and embel-
lished stories, throughout the rest of the book. The inclusion
of the "real" next to the fictional (ornamented speeches,
poems, riddles, emblems, songs) is perfectly consistent with
the author's announced intent of presenting the multifaceted
nature of literature.

Ironically this factuality is also a way to attract attention
to the very artistry and literary effort involved in the cultivation of pastoral art. If the real is also going to be included,
than things have to be presented in a way that is not the same
as those "remembered" by the storyteller and carefully retold in euphemic terms. A different use and arrangement of
language must follow. In this particular case, we have a story
that, in its economy, conciseness, and brevity, reflects the
unexpected and rapid nature of events in real life. There are
no hyperboles, pleonasms, repetitions, metaphors to "reflect" empirical happenings. What gives this episode its striking force is the absence of rhetorical elaboration. The difference between this and the surrounding stories make it particularly evident.

---

(36) *Ibid.*, Libro Primero, p. 28.

After the "factual" episode has ended, the commentator resumes his place, alternating with the voices of the characters. Lisandro, Carino's killer, explains to Elicio and Erastro the reason for his action, becoming a character, narrator, and commentator on the little vignette and on his own tale. Now, however, and consistent with the rhetorical conventions and expectations of the genre, the speaker will resume his narration in terms of ordinary pastoral rhetoric.

In love with Leonida, Lisandro plans their elopement and secret marriage without their respective families' consent. Aided by Silvia, Leonida's friend, they arrange to leave town one night and travel to a relative's home. Grisalvo, Leonida's brother and Silvia's fiancé, learns of the plan through Carino, to whom Silvia had confided in requesting his help. The jealous Carino, seeking revenge, deceives them all. Leonida dies at her own brother's hands; and lovers, families, and towns are destroyed by Carino's malicious plot.

The story, thematically, is a new version of a classical and enduring fable: Piramo and Thisbe's tragic love. In *La Galatea*, this episode also reflects and contains, in a concentrated form, many of the larger stories, themes, and subplots later developed in the rest of the book. By playing with the similarities of characters' names in this and other stories (Grisalvo here and Grisaldo in Book Four), with the sibling relationships (Leonida/Grisalvo here, Teolinda/Leonarda later in the same First Book and Nisida/Blanca in Books Two and Five), and by placing the story in a parallel position with that of Teolinda and Artidoro, Cervantes accomplishes the compression and interweaving characteristic of the work.

Teolinda's Tale

As in Lisandro's narrative, Teolinda's tells a story to an internal audience in the Book. Just as Elicio and Erastro were the listeners in the case of the tragic story, so Galatea and Florisa are the sympathetic audience for this contrastive tale.

— 153 —

Both the thematic content and tone create contrast since Teolinda is at first indifferent to love. It also contrasts in length because Teolinda's, unlike Lisandro's, exceeds indeed the frame of the First Book. At the request of Galatea and Florisa (herself a model of eloquence, discretion, and beauty), and over her initial promise of reticence ("No sé cómo pagaros si no es con callar."), Teolinda tells her story in great detail.

Yo, que a lo último quedaba, y que allí deudo alguno no tenía, mostrando hacer de la desenvuelta, me llegué al forastero pastor y poniéndole una guirnalda en la cabeza le dije: "Esta te doy buen zagal, por dos cosas; la una por el contento que a todos nos has dado con tu agradable canto; la otra, porque en nuestra aldea se usa honrrar a los extranjeros"... Yo no sé cómo en tan pequeño espacio de tiempo me transformé en otro ser del que tenía, porque yo no vivía en mí, sino en Artidoro, que ansí se llama la mitad de mi alma que ando buscando...[Artidoro] comenzó a cantar unos versos que . . . hasta agora no se me han olvidado y . . . os los habré de decir, que son estos:

En áspera, cerrada, escura noche,
sin ver jamás el esperado día
y en continuo crecido amargo llanto,
ajeno de placer, contento y risa,
merece estar, y en una viva muerte,
aquel que sin amor pasa la vida. (37)

. . . A este punto del cuento de sus amores llegaba Teolinda, cuando las pastoras sintieron grandísimo estruendo de

---

(37) This *sestina* in praise of love (that is, the sorrows and pleasures of love) is, as the one analyzed in Chapter V, a double sextine as well as a modified one. Here, the second stanza is irregular, but it follows the night/day, life/death opposites of the Petrarchean models.

voces de pastores y ladridos de perros que fue causa que
dejasen la comenzada plática. (38)

Once again, there is at the end of the Libro Primero a
brief, emblem-like episode that, repeating the theme of pursuit in a symmetrical echo of the earlier hunter and the
hunted, serves to bring Galatea to the fore as a catalyst, an
intermediary who rescues the exhausted hare from the teeth
of the hounds and certain death. Interestingly as well, both
this scene and Teolinda's tale are interrupted by Galatea's
father who, at the end of the book, interferes with Galatea's
own sentimental life (39).

The importance of Teolinda's story, inserted between very
different and contrastive ones, lies partly in the fact that her
love story reflects versions presented by other characters
(Lenio, Gelasia) and that it contrasts with the faithfulness
and dedication portrayed in the other stories in the other
books (i.e. Nisida, Blanca, Timbrio, Silerio). But structurally,
the story of her love for Artidoro with its many vicissitudes
serves to maintain a continuous thread that alternatively appears and is hidden in the background book after book. A
similar effect is achieved by the use of poetic compositions in
carefully designed repetitions, such as the sextine of Artidoro,
recited by Teolinda, that is repeated in Book Five in a sonnet
sung by Erastro:

Erastro:

Por ásperos caminos voy siguiendo
el fin dudoso de mi fantasía,

---

(38) *La Galatea*, Avalle-Arce, editor, Libro Primero, pp. 62-79.
(39) The commentator says: "Mas Galatea, tomando la temerosa
liebre en los brazos, estorbó su intento a los cobdiciosos perros." This
vignette was used again as an emblem by Cervantes in *Don Quijote* (II,
LXXIII). For don Quijote, the hare turned out to be a negative sign.
Ibid., Libro Primero, p. 79.

siempre en cerrada noche escura y fría
las fuerzas de la vida consumiendo.

Y aunque morir me veo, no pretendo
salir un paso de la estrecha vía:
que en fe de la alta fe sin igual mía,
mayores miedos contrastar entiendo.

Mi fe es la luz que me señala el puerto . . . (40)

With the line—"en áspera, cerrada, escura noche"—the text recited by Teolinda (quoted from the person who first composed it) creates a web of intertextual connections of importance in the poetics of *La Galatea*. The connections, allowed precisely by the convention of recuperation by repetition, results in an associative evocation for the reader. The repeated words are now part of the reader's *habitude*. Previous and present texts are thus united and transformed in a new text. Here, the remembrance of one book is reinforced (Book One) through another (Book Five). And, as Avalle-Arce notes in his edition, the words and sonnet echo the sonnet and words of Garcilaso in his soneto VI: "Por ásperos caminos ha llegado" (41). Teolinda's quoted *sestina*, in turn, recuperates the basic thematic oppositions of noche/día, muerte/vida of the earlier and famous sestinas, by Petrarch among others (42).

From a thematic point of view, however, her story carries a greater weight since it reflects in many respects the story of Nisida/Blanca and, more important, that of Galatea. Exploiting the convention of repetition, similarity, and reflection, Cervantes uses the diverse characters to reflect and/or shield

---

(40) *Ibid.*, Libro Quinto, p. 142.
(41) *Ibid.*, p. 142, note 2.
(42) Francesco Petrarca, *Canzoniere*, ed. by Aldo Garzanti, Milano, 1974, p. 118.

other characters who, in this fashion, keep their mystery, importance, or effect. This is precisely the case of Galatea, who is shielded by Teolinda here but whose presence as audience and rescuer of the hare makes of her the point of reference.

Characterization, Intertextuality, and Structure

One of the most obvious features of the novel, is the elusiveness and scarcity of appearance of the supposed main character of the story throughout. This was also the case of the protagonist in Montemayor's *Diana*. Yet Galatea's presence is constantly felt in her role as witness or through the allusions of her admirers and their poems dedicated to her and the discourses and descriptions supplied by the narrator. She is witness, audience, and agent in the previously mentioned episodes, and later, in the stories of Blanca (Libro Quinto) and of Silveria (Libros Tercero and Cuarto).

As with those other shepherdesses, her true feelings are rather ambiguous. The impression left in the reader is primarily of the rhetorical persuasiveness and mystery contained in the retelling of their pleasurable sorrows rather than a sense of the disclosure of the shepherdesses' true selves; that is, their beautiful words conceal their inner feelings. Yet, there is here, both in Galatea and Teolinda (one of Galatea's reflections) an attempt at characterization that makes these two more appealing. This attempt is one of the innovations of *La Galatea*, and it remains true even if the figures of Teolinda and Galatea maintain their roles as epitomes of beauty and models of perfection.

The similarities between them are not created by an association of names (as is the case of Galatea, Blanca, and Silveria), nor by any link in their sentimental situation. It is instead made via artistic accumulation of shades of meaning and detail as they progress from their initial stance—aloof, controlled—toward the vulnerability and complexity that adds depth to them. As in the case of other model shepherdesses, Galatea combines beauty, discretion, eloquence (or reticence), elegance, and charm. As she was introduced by the commentator, explaining the feelings of Elicio, she is of incomparable beauty, and "de tan alto y subido entendimento que las discretas damas en los reales palacios . . . se tuvieran por dichosas de parecerla en algo, asi en la discreción como en la hermosura" (43).

Teolinda, "pastora de gentil donaire y apostura," is addressed by Galatea with the words: "Asi los cielos, hermosa pastora, se muestren favorables a lo que pedirles quisieres . . ." and by Florisa, "Con ninguna cosa, discreta zagala, satisfarás más nuestros deseos . . . que con darnos cuenta de lo que te hemos rogado" (44).

But as Teolinda is beautiful, so she is also fickle, full of spontaneity, and wit: "mostrando hacer la desenvuelta," she approaches the shepherd and starts an acquaintance under the pretense of explaining local customs, "Porque en nuestra aldea se usa honrar a los estranjeros." Like this resourceful shepherdess, Galatea, as reported in the first pages of the book, avoided conversation with Elicio and Erastro with a fib.

The combination of refinement and spontaneity is one of the characteristics that sets Galatea, and her reflection Teolinda, apart from the majority of the characters of the book. They are models of perfection as the formulaic language employed to address them attests ("discreta," "hermosa," "gentil"), and as proven by the admiration and praise devoted to them by the poet/shepherds. They are also spontaneous sometimes, a quality that brings them closer to the empathy of the audience. This combination of refinement and "naturalness" is one more instance of the effort to pre-

---

(43) *La Galatea,* Avalle-Arce, editor, Libro Primero, p. 16.
(44) *Ibid.,* pp. 61, 62, and 65.

sent a variety of facets as a central poetic aim, announced by Cervantes with his metaphor of the broken mirror. It is also, in an analogous sense, a way to link Galatea's role with that of poetry as a theme. Like pastoral poetry (itself a combination of vernacular and classical roots, of prose and verse), Galatea is seen in a variety of roles. She is the inspiration, audience, and confidant of the other shepherds (poets). As the emblem-like episode of the hare illustrates, she is also the refuge for the fatigued. And as Teolinda and she later demonstrate, she is the cause and the cure not only of feelings but of the exercise of persuasive, narrative discourse.

Thus in Book Five, when Galatea is finally more openly revealed and participates more fully in discourses and songs, we learn that her voice acts as a drug or a magic spell:

> . . . *No anduvieron mucho cuando llegó a sus oidos la zampoña de Florisa, acompañada de la voz de Galatea, que como de los pastores fue oĭda, quedaron enajenados de sĭ mesmos.* (45)

But later, after the audience listens to the perfection of her poem in *redondillas* (pp. 133, 134, "¿A quién volveré los ojos/ en el mal que se apareja/ si cuanto mi bien se aleja/ se acercan más mis enojos?") and the reasoned arguments with which she defends her problematic loyalties, she is seen as "el sol que nos alumbra" (that is, almost as a deity or indeed a star) "la discreción que nos admira" and "la belleza que los incita y anima a mil honrosas competencias" (46). Later on, she is also held to be a new miracle of beauty (47), but moving to yet another level, she is also held to be human and therefore subject to sadness and defeat (at her father's command):

---

(45) *Ibid.*, Libro Quinto, p. 132.
(46) *Ibid.*, Libro Sexto, p. 137.
(47) *Ibid.*, p. 167.

> *Y abrazando a todos los que con Elicio quedaban, se fueron con Aurelio, con el cual iban Florisa, Teolinda y Maurisa, y la triste Galatea, tan acongojada y pensativa, que con toda su discreción no podía dejar de dar muestras de estraño descontento.* (48)

Even at the moment where her possible destiny is going to be decided and in spite of the seeming exhaustion of the multi-faceted versions of her role, Galatea remains mysterious, elusive, and wrapped in a cloak of strangeness.

Through the frequent, episodic appearances in the text, sometimes lengthy, sometimes brief, and as a listener, narrator, emblem, or reflection of other similar fictional lives (i.e. Teolinda here and Nísida/Blanca in other books) Galatea has been a constant, yet not a definitive character. "El no se qué" (Book Two, p. 90) surrounding Galatea, and the characteristic tag expression in Teolinda's speech "Yo no sé cómo deciros" becomes consistent once more with Galatea as a simile for the description of art, the "tercera naturaleza a la cual no sabré dar nombre," as Telesio refers to it later in Book Six (49).

Thus Galatea's story is reflected in that of Teolinda as it is in other episodes, stories, and Libros, which are built according to a system of juxtapositions giving the book an uneven, nested configuration. This structuring of stories within stories (the adaptation of the convention of *amplificatio* in pastoral narratives) has an obvious retardatory function. Complicated presentation delays not only the revelation of Galatea's character, but also any solution to her riddle-like situation. In this case Cervantes exploits the convention to a maximum degree, perhaps thereby involving the audience even further in the development of the story.

There are in *La Galatea* recognizable, basic strategies common to other pastorals (*La Diana, El Pastor de Fílida, Ar-*

---

(48) *Ibid.*, p. 167.
(49) *Ibid.*, p. 170.

cadia). For example, a "discreta," elusive, extremely beautiful maiden, is subject of the plot. Torn by conflict between the inclination of her affections and external forces (time, fortune, society, or parental demands) her conflict is made explicit, but not clearly solved by artful and equally complicated verbal discourse using different narrative techniques. The narrative, thus artfully composed of nesting elements, contrasts, similes, and metaphors within equivalent or contrastive arrangements in the work, delays in the solution of the hero/heroine's situation and also accumulates levels of information which the audience ponders and judges. To work, the conventions of the genre require a re-elaboration of well-established models, expressions, and themes that the audiences recognize and associate with those of earlier works of the genre, but the re-elaboration has to be done in accordance with the work's internal harmony.

In the case of *La Galatea*, all the resources and technical aspects are extremely complicated but are ultimately integrated within the whole text. Taking any one of the stories, themes, or expressions and following it through the work, we find that the units are arranged to reflect and complement each other to the smallest detail. In the way these tales are integrated with the means of expression, the audience can measure the effect and eloquence of each one of the passages, just as the individual narrators of the internal plot measure each story against the one told by somebody else. In this Cervantine version of pastoral, the interaction between the stories told and the means of expression makes evident the difference between fiction and reality. Even when fiction appears to be simple, devoid of artifice, it can never dismiss complexity. One of the ways to deal with this complexity is the pastoral "laying bare" technique of reflecting the multiplicity of aspects as in a broken mirror.

Intertextuality and Characterization in Book Two

The Libro Segundo begins with the continuation of Teolinda's story where all audiences learn how Artidoro won her heart, and how indiscretion (uncertainty and deceit) on her part complicated their situation to an almost tragic point. It is with the persuasion of his words, his poems written on the bark of trees (pp. 99-101), her songs (pp. 92, 104) that Artidoro and Teolinda, as other lovers in former pastorals ("doces amarillys silvas" of Virgil's Eclogue I) communicated their love. It was because of the lack of words—her concealment and deceit—that Leonarda, Teolinda's twin sister misinterpreted the situation, setting the events on a more complicated course. But it is also by the interpolation of the commentator's words that the story is interrupted and a new segment is introduced. This interruption, a technique already used in other forms of literature, i.e. epic and in chivalric novels, as well as in earlier pastorals (*Arcadia, La Diana*, and Gálvez de Montalvo's *Pastor de Filida*, among others) has here a retardatory effect. In addition, by lack of continuity; by unfinished explanation—the story takes a more complicated course. The sentence, interjected by the commentator, serves as one of the cues for a change of theme and a transition to a new scene.

In the particular case of the Libro Segundo, the sentence introduces two new shepherds, Damon and Tirsi, whose music, stories, and artistry from an equivalent parallel with that of Elicio and in many sentimental aspects with that of Erastro as well. From a literary point of view, these two poets are re-incarnations of well-known shepherds who, echoing each other's verses and songs, give a two-sided version of their common pastoral complaint. There has been a prestigious literary line of dialoguing shepherds since Theocritus' *Idylls* (Tyrsis and the Goatherd in Idyll I, Lacon and Comatas of Idyll V, and Daphnis and Menalcas of Idyll IX), the shepherds of Virgil's *Eclogues* (Meliboeus and Tirsi, I and Corydon and Mopsus VII, as well as in Idylls III, V, and IX), and closer to the time and literary tradition of Cervantes, the sweetly melancholic poets of Garcilaso's *Eglogas* (especially Eglogas I and III) as well as the shepherds of *La Diana*.

An intertextual connection with the lineage of those literary shepherds is further stressed in *La Galatea* in a way that makes evident Cervantes' experimentation with the possibilities of the conventions of the pastoral genre. Tirsi and Damon in this renewed version not only resemble earlier cases, but they speak identical words. In their first appearance in the text, they repeat the same lines Garcilaso's shepherds used in his *Eglogas*. Damon, as he addresses his own Amarili in *La Galatea*, says:

> *Oh más que el cielo, oh más que el sol hermosa,*
> *y para mi más dura que un diamante,*
> *presta a mi mal, y al bien muy perezosa*
> *   ¿Cuál ábrego, cuál cierzo, cuál levante*
> *te sopló de aspereza, que así ordenas . . .?* (50)

And later on, the same Damon adds in a sonnet:

> *Más blando fui que no la blanda cera,*
> *cuando imprimi en mi alma la figura*
> *de la bella Amarili, esquiva y dura*
> *cual duro mármol o silvestre fiera* (51)

Recent and earlier readers (52) of pastoral have identified these with identical words sung by Tirreno, one of the shepherds in Garcilaso's Egloga I: " ¡Oh más dura que mármol a mis quejas/ y al encendido fuego en que me quemo/ más

---

(50) *Ibid.*, p. 109.
(51) *Ibid.*, p. 120.
(52) Cf. *ibid.*, p. 109, n. 2.

helada que nieve, Galatea" (53). And as I noted previously in Chapter III, the lines that Damon recites here are also an echo of Montemayor's shepherd Sylvano who in the Livro II of *La Diana* had sung:

> *Pastora mǐa, más blanca y colorada*
> *que ambas rosas por abril cogidas,*
> *y más resplandeciente*
>
> *que el sol que de oriente*
> *por la mañana asoma a tu majada.* (54)

The author of *La Galatea*, acting as a reader and interpreter of those earlier lines, is incorporating—almost fusing—here the words of his characters into the same lineage (language) of shepherds that belong to the pastoral. In so doing and by the act of quoting other authors and other shepherds verbatim or with slight alteration of tone, he identifies his characters with those inhabitants of the literary pastorals. Quoting masters of the genre, borrowing whole lines, the pastoral shepherd/poets become someone else. They not only repeat what they say but they *are* the other.

This identification takes on additional dimensions in the present case for, as many critics have already noted (55), these disguised shepherds, Tirsi and Damon are in real life the poets Francisco de Figueroa and Pedro Lainez respectively. This fact is further supported—and the game of disguises further complicated—when the supposed shepherds as well as their friends, quote their own lines and repeat verses from their own published works. This is the case of

---

(53) Garcilaso de la Vega, *Obras*, Madrid, Espasa-Calpe, Austral, 1961, "Egloga I," vv. 57-59, p. 26.

(54) Jorge de Montemayor, *Los siete libros de la Diana*, cited ed., Livro Segundo, p. 277.

(55) Cf. Jas. Fitzmaurice-Kelly, *op. cit.*, "Introduction," also, Avalle-Arce, *La novela pastoril española*, p. 104.

Elicio who, recognizing Tirsi/Figueroa, the famous shepherd from Compluto, addresses him with quotations from Figueroa's own work:

> *Ay Tirsi, Tirsi—respondió Elicio. . . . No sé yo cómo viene bien lo que tu agora dices con lo que un tiempo decĭas cuando cantabas: —¡Ay, de cuán ricas esperanzas vengo!* (56)

And Erastro—whom some critics, accepting his own self-deprecatory disclaimers, have given the role of the *rustic*— says:

> *No tienes que maravillarte de lo que Elicio ha dicho, ni él tampoco de lo que tú dices, ni traer por ejemplo aquello que él dice que cantabas, ni menos lo que yo sé que cantaste cuando dijiste:*
>
> *"La amarillez y la flaqueza mĭa,"*
> . . . .

[and] *. . . en aquellos versos tan nombrados tuyos, que si mal no recuerdo comenzaban:*

> *"Sale el* [sic] *aurora, y de su fértil manto."* (57)

In addition to the interest that this complicated game of recognition of relationships with earlier texts arouses, identification is significant from a structural point of view. The discourse as a whole takes the form of a two-part harmony (Elicio and Erastro echoing Tirsi and Damon) whose resolution and finale occurs in the Libro Cuarto after each one of the pair of shepherds—sister/brother, couples of lovers—finds each other to be equivalent or correspondent, thus closing

---

(56) *La Galatea*, Avalle-Arce, editor, Libro Segundo, p. 116.
(57) *Ibid.*, p. 117.

the circle of their story within the larger frame of the plot. Thus Teolinda is reunited with Artidoro, Tirsi and Damon find the sympathetic echo in the equally sorrowful and unrequited Elicio and Erastro (although they do not solve their sentimental problems), Timbrio and Silerio find their respective Nísida and Blanca, and Daranio is united with Silveria.

The pairs, in correspondence with other characters and other episodes of the work, move from Book Two to Book Four. But with the exception of the wedding of the rich Daranio to the shepherdess Silveria, there is no clear resolution of their sentimental problems. Even in the wedding, doubt remains for, though Daranio is happy with the marriage, Silveria had given her word and heart to a younger but impecunious man.

The movement is maintained not only by inclusion of those shepherds and the story of Teolinda which proceeds after a physical interruption in the text but is also further maintained by the insertion of a much larger and more complicated story first initiated immediately after the audience gets acquainted with the songs, art, and situation of Tirsi and Damon. As they talk about their friendship and connection with the other main characters in the preceding scenes, Florisa, Galatea, and Teolinda are hidden, thus being a secret audience. After they reveal their presence and join the shepherds in their discourse, they all become the audience of Silerio who disguised as a hermit has been hiding in a nearby chapel or shrine. His story is entitled "Los dos amigos."

Two children of prominent families of the city of Jerez, Timbrio and Silerio, grew up together. Caught between love and loyalty, they endure challenges that test their strength and friendship to the limit. At the end they conquer adversity, becoming the epitome of friendship: "los dos amigos."

The setting for this adventure-filled episode is interesting and not only because of the enormous influence that its themes already had in peninsular literature and were later to have after Cervantes' repeated adaptations of the tale. This long and complex story of friendship tested by love, love tested by time, and fortune tested by repeated instances of human deceit (pp. 148, 158, 154, 176) presents a perfect opportunity to experiment with new levels of narrative. In the case of Cervantes' readaptation, these opportunities are taken advantage of to the fullest extent.

One of the most noticeable characteristics of this version of the tale is that the voice of the character Silerio, as narrator of his own story, makes possible transformations that the outside narrator could not exercise. Because Silerio narrates his own story, he can supposedly present to the audiences the close view of the "insider." However his repeated deceptions ("Asi, sin descubrirse ni imaginarse mi industria, vine a salir con mi primero designio, que era facilitar la entrada en casa de Nísida . . . Admirado quedé de la discreta traza de Nísida, y aún no sin sospecha de la verdad de mi artificio"), obfuscations (58), and disguises make it obvious to the reader that he, as a storyteller, is arranging the story carefully, "artistically."

Thus, in addition to the prolongation by detail, digressions, quoted letters (59), secondary episodes, and songs—all common in other types of literature as well—Silerio uses rhetorical means (i.e. hyperboles) to characterize her in a way that would both persuade his audience and satisfy their expectations as readers of the pastoral. This is, for instance, how Nísida, the object of constant inspiration of the two *amigos'* love, is presented:

Su nombre era Nísida, y su hermosura tanta, que me atrevo a decir que la naturaleza cifró en ella el extremo de sus perfecciones, y . . . tan a una en ella la honestidad y la belleza, que lo que la una encendía la otra enfriaba, y los deseos

---

(58) *Ibid.*, pp. 145, 153, 156.
(59) *Ibid.*, pp. 152-153.

que su gentileza hasta el más subido cielo levantaba, su
honesta gravedad hasta lo más bajo de la tierra abatía. (60)

Nísida, a reflection of the other familiar shepherdesses already introduced in the text, is described by her admirer in the expectedly hyperbolic terms of pastoral. As in previous cases, "the extremes of her perfections" makes of this privileged creature an epitome equal only to the models that she reflects.

In other words, Cervantes, conforming to the expectations required by the conventions and by the readers, uses the conventions exactly as they are supposed to be used. Ironically, these repetitions, in their sameness, actually stress the differences conveyed by other means. In this case, Nísida is as hyperbolically beautiful as Galatea and Teolinda before, but the rhythm, the tone and disposition of her story and above all the actual process of her presentation invites the audiences to compare and to derive distinctions between them. Nísida, unlike the two other heroines, narrators and active participants in their own fate, remains unchanged through the course of the book. Her story enmeshed with that of the two friends is presented in such a complex and multifaceted way that, although Nísida is in a prominent place as an object of the narrator's affections, there are a number of related, intertwined stories and themes that are of equal importance. Thus the themes of friendship, parental opposition (as in *Piramo and Thisbe* and *Romeo and Juliet*), pirates and thieves (Books II and III), abduction, shipwrecks, loyalty (Nísida and her sister Blanca) are related and equated to each other and to similar stories in the rest of the book.

From a structural point of view, this complex episode—the longest of those inserted in the *Galatea*—is important for its window-like composition with multiple panes of glass, as it were. In this interesting structure, the voice of the narrator

(60) *Ibid.*, p. 121.

makes evident the organized and organic arrangement of the discourse. In the long interrupted, reconstructed, and recounted tale, this character/narrator seems to delight at times in the effect that the telling or reading (i.e. of letters), singing, and reciting of poems has on his audience as well as on himself. The voice seems stimulated by the act of narrating and by the power of persuasion that the artful storyteller can have. In this sense, the narrator's voice is conscious of the effect that the convention of eurhythmia, harmony, and eloquence has in the rhetoric of pastoral and conscious also of the delay those devices provide (61).

Silerio's story, although lengthy and developed during the large part of the Libro Segundo, does not conclude with the end of the book but continues through the Libro Tercero and Cuarto to finally close some of its sub-stories in the Libro Quinto. Although some of the stories already recounted in the second book are, as pointed out, reflections or parallels with other stories in the novel as a whole, the reflection that the story carries forward most clearly is a reflection on itself. Thus the first internal audience (i.e. Silerio addressing the shepherds Elicio, Erastro, Tirsi, Damon, Galatea, Florisa, and Teolinda) acts as a larger frame within which the multiple, related levels of the narration subsequently occur. But within that larger, though equally fictional frame, secondary episodes are reflected: e.g. the first act of loyalty between

---

(61) Eurythmia, or what Cicero called *numerus*, as a reglatory rhetorical principle, emphasizes a proper balance of the elements of the sentence. The effects of a persuasive discourse are to be reckoned with, as the dog Berganza pointed out when referring to the effects of the patoral discourses. These "well-worded" tales, obfuscate the mind, he says, transporting the speaker—and the audience—to another level, out-of-the-discourse: "Agradézcotelo, Cipión, amigo, por que si no me avisaras, de manera se me iba calentando la boca, que no parara hasta pintarte un libro entero de estos que me tenian engañado." Miguel de Cervantes, *Novelas ejemplares*, ed. by Leonardo G. de Morelos, Garden City, N.Y., Doubleday & Co. Inc., 1962, pp. 458 459.

the friends at the beginning is mirrored in a similar act in the middle and at the end; the capture by a gang of thieves in Libro Segundo is mirrored by the capture by pirates in Libro Tercero. The general effect is that of a mirror within a mirror, or a prism that reflects light in multiple ways. The experiment is, thus, a small resume of the six books of *La Galatea*, as they are reflected within the frame of an inserted episode.

Structure and Language in Libro Tercero, Cuarto, and Quinto

Book Three begins as a continuation of the previous development. This beginning makes its development an unfinished, partial sequel, an anticipation of other books and of other themes. Anticipations of events to come, such as the frustrated, sentimental wishes of Galatea, are found in the brief, bittersweet vignette of Silveria's wedding (p. 178) and in remembrances of episodes already recounted (the tragedy of Leonida and Grisalvo, p. 185) which are intertwined in loose, fluid balance with the continuing narration of "Los dos amigos" tale.

Although each one of these larger and smaller episodes is worthy of closer scrutiny, the constraints of my subject dictate that I close the reading of these stories with a special reference to the episode that in turn serves to close the narrative of the third book.

As part of Silveria's wedding to Daranio, and as counter-comment on the unequal quality of love that the couple represents, four shepherds (Orompo, Marsilio, Crisio, and Orfinio) stage an Eclogue in the true manner of pastoral. The group of shepherd/poets at the wedding attend as a literal audience of the representation of this musical vignette which is itself an echo of pastorals of the past. As the shepherds —and similarly-named poets—of Sanazzaro's *Arcadia*, this group of "enamorados y de amor oprimidos pastores" sing their eclogue, a recapitulation of the sorrows of unrequited love.

Of special interest, besides the recuperation of characters and conventional formulas that this foursome represents, is the language and the meters of versification used in their songs. They use Petrarchean images, and repeat Italian verses, but in keeping with the rural setting of the Spanish wedding, they combine them with Castilian compositions that had been relegated to secondary levels ever since the "itálico modo" of the meters introduced by Garcilaso and Boscán. In this way the *Coplas de arte mayor* (ABBAACCA) sung by Orompo are to be understood.

Salid de lo hondo del pecho cuitado
palabras sangrientas, con muerte mezcladas;
y si los sospiros os tienen atadas,
abrid y romped el siniestro costado

El aire os impide, que está ya inflamado
del fiero veneno de vuestros acentos
salid, y siquiera os lleven los vientos,

que todo mi bien tambien me han llevado ... (62)

As Avalle-Arce notes (63), there is a great deal of love of tradition in the choice of such a typically Spanish meter. This is both love for the national traditions and the need to maintain the verisimilitude of the scenes, the themes, and the linguistic details. I would add, that this recuperation is an intentional part of the pastoral and as is the cultivation of a national art, together with other innovations following from contemporary and classical literatures. Thus the intended aim announced by the prologue is realized in a variety of ways,

---

(62) *La Galatea,* Avalle-Arce, editor, Libro Tercero, p. 205.
(63) *Ibid.,* p. 205, note 13.

themes, and structural forms (once again the idea of the "roto espejo o por arte compuesto"). It is in this same light that I read the insertion of some proverbs and riddles, both at the end of Libro Tercero and later again, as a reflection, at the end of Libro Sexto.

To experiment with diverse formulas and means of expression is consistent with Cervantes' definition of art: "el arte no se aventaja a la naturaleza sino perfecciónala." This concern, demonstrated endlessly, throughout this, his first literary composition, is repeated and discussed in the rest of the work (64). So too do the riddles and the proverbs symmetrically placed at the end of the third and sixth books. They illustrate the effort to present the variety of aspects and degrees included in literary art; that is, mixed with the refined language of the imported meters of versification (sonnet, sextine, ottava rima) are the songs and ballads of the vernacular tradition (at Daranio's wedding for instance). Added to those forms, and as proof perhaps of the versatility provided by the aesthetics of the genre, Cervantes includes here proverbs and riddles, product of commonsense wisdom and non-literary speech.

As a continuation of the internal dialectic of these six partitions of *La Galatea*, Libro Cuarto develops and enlarges the themes and aspects announced in the preceding Libro Tercero, as well as in episodes of the previous books. The story of Teolinda and Artidoro, for instance, interrupted by the unceasing intrusions of other narratives and other events, is continued and complicated by their reunion and the secondary effects of it. The complications are partially due to the fact that both Teolinda and Artidoro have doubles, literal competitors in the persons of their respective identical twins. Their story is also complicated by their accidental separation

---

(64) E. C. Riley dedicates an illuminating discussion to this particular Cervantine concern. See Riley, *op. cit.*, pp. 69 and ff. Also in *Don Quijote*, II, XVI, cited edition, p. 650.

which gives room for other commitments and other sentimental entanglements as a result of the original confusion and deceit.

These complications achieve a delaying effect. There are also additional advantages such as the inclusion of secondary characters (Artandro, Rosaura, Leopersia) which further echo, mirror, and reflect upon the larger stories and the subsequent development of events. In some cases, it is by the play on linguistic similarities—Rosaura is in love with Grisaldo echo of Grisalvo in Book One; Leonarda, Teolinda's twin is like Leopersia a victim of confusion (though not as tragic as that of the Leonida of the First Book. Thus Leonarda, Leopersia and Leonida are echoing each other's story and each other's name. At other times, and in contrast with the sequence of other tales, the audience learns first of the reunion of two lovers—of whom no one had direct knowledge—and then we learn the rest of their story through one or several narrators' words. Rosaura's story, for instance, is presented in this order. Both in this Libro Cuarto and in the Libros Primero and Segundo, the figure of the unrequited, lonely, almost desperate shepherd passes through the narratives as a counterpoint, or a motto in other expressive arts: Lenio (Libros Primero and Segundo), Mireno (Libro Tercero) and Lauso (Libro Quinto), as well as Gelasia (Libro Quinto). They serve as leit-motiv, illustrating by contrast or similarity the mysteries of love.

In the Libro Quinto the conclusions of some stories are suspended and the ambiguity of the situations is stressed. However, and perhaps by virtue of the suspension itself, the true subject of the stories and discourses themselves is the power of words. In prominent, but not exclusive place are the words of consolation, as directed to the "discretos" Erastro and Elicio (p. 126) and to the happier Timbrio by the no less "discreto" Aurelio:

Se han quedado con él, Elicio y Erastro y yo he venido
a darte las nuevas del término que le tienen sus pensa-
mientos. Y pues a ti te son manifiestos, procura remediar-
los con obras, o acude a consolarlos con palabras. (65)

Equally caught up in the power of the rhetoric and by the
persuasion of which they are now perfectly aware, the shepherds put an end to the interrupted tale of the nautical ad-
venture but not to the pursuit of their destinies. These seem
to be dependent solely on the power of the communicative
discourse which in this case is information:

Con estas últimas palabras dio fin a su cuento el alegre
Timbrio . . . pasando el contento de Silerio a todo lo que
decir se puede, el cual tornando de nuevo a abrazar a
Timbrio, forzado del deseo de saber . . . se apartó con
Timbrio a una parte, donde supo dél que la hermosa
Blanca. (66)

The story of Blanca, betrothed against her will to the gentle-
man Darinto, parallels the story of Galatea who, at the end
of this same book, learns of her father's decision to marry her
off to a rich, mysterious *caballero* from Portugal, and here
the audience receives this information.

But all the stories—sad (as with these two shepherdesses),
happy (Timbrio and Silerio's reunion), desperate (Lauso's
attempted suicide), and of consolatory intent (Aurelio, Elicio,
and Erastro consoling Lauso, Tirsi, and Damon)—are a display and constant comment on the power of discourse and
speech. This emphasis is carried forward to such an extent
that on practically every page of this Fifth Book, there is
some reference to the power of discourse and of linguistic
art.

(65) *La Galatea,* Avalle-Arce, editor, Libro Quinto, p. 126.
(66) *Ibid.,* p. 122.

In addition to the arguments in the passages cited, we find that words are dangerous if used to reveal what one wants to keep secret. Words can be used—or omitted—to keep control of information and to conceal inner feelings.

> *Abrió Elicio los ojos y porque conoció a todos los que allí estaban, tuvo cuenta que con su lengua, movida y forzada del dolor, no dijese algo que la causa dél manifestate.* (p. 128)

By the same token, words, even when used in large quantities, can serve a persuasive intent:

> *. . . Acude a colsolarlos con palabras. —Palabras serán todas, buen Aurelio—respondió Timbrio, las que yo en esto gastaré.* (p. 126)

But there are cases when the power of even a great amount of words does not suffice:

> *Comenzó* [Damón] *a consolar a Elicio; pero todas sus palabras en ser palabras quedaban sin que ningún otro efecto hiciesen.* (p. 131)

That limitation of the power of words is, nevertheless, balanced when words are expressed by the heroine herself. Her words, as already mentioned above, have the effect of a drug that causes madness via alienation:

> *Llegó a sus oidos . . . la voz de la hermosa Galatea que, como de los pastores fue oída, quedaron enajenados de sí mesmos.* (p. 132)

And words can also be used as promises, i.e. legal contracts ("me atreva a cumplir con las obras lo que con palabras te ofrezco," p. 137), betrothal or vows ("ha dado palabra de ser la esposa de Artandro," p. 139), artistic communication (the "redondillas" sung by Galatea, pp. 133-134), repetition and recuperation of earlier words (Erastro's sonnet: "Por ásperos caminos," p. 142), and dialogue and narration (pp. 143-145). They are also vehicles of reticence ("No se acertaban a decir palabra," p. 126), illusion, and grammatical exercise.

These grammatical exercises, used for different purposes, are accomplished by several means. Examples are paranomasia, conjugation of verbs, pleonasm, formulaic address, ellipsis, pathetic fallacy, and fixed expressions or clichés. The following quotation contains examples:

> *Advierte que lo que te **suplico** es tan conforme y llegado a razón, que **irĭas de todo en todo** fuera della si no me lo **concedieses**. Porque, ¡qué ley ordena, o qué razón consiente que la hermosura que nosotros criamos, la discreción que en estas selvas y aldeas nuestras tuvo principio, el donaire por particular don del cielo a nuestra patria concedido . . . se haya de llevar a extraños reinos . . .? ¡Oh verdes prados . . . ¡Oh flores olorosas . . . ¡Oh plantas, oh árboles desta deleitosa selva!* (p. 143, emphasis mine)

The extreme of the shepherd's sorrow at the departure of Galatea makes him emphasize his feelings by repetitions of formulas (suplico), of words (such as the pleonasm "do todo en todo"), and the repeated use of the pathetic fallacy (" ioh verdes prados, ioh flores . . . haced todo en la mejor forma que pudiéredes . . ."). But the exteriorization of his exacerbated state also makes him use ellipsis ("llegado a razón, que *irĭas* de todo en todo fuera della"), although as we saw earlier (see footnote 33), ellipsis are often used to accomplish other aims.

Of interest in these pages, as proven by the debates generated, are instances of fixed expressions, clichés which, as in the case of the pleonastic "de todo en todo," are inserted as part of an emotional speech. In such cases, the well-known expression reinforces the argument pursued (i.e. to reach a consensus about keeping Galatea among the internal audience of the shepherds). In other instances, the use of the cliché ("Sí, respondió Florisa—; *que yo segura que*, ante que la noche llegue, él tenga dél noticia," p. 141, emphasis mine) is in function of some reassuring intent (67).

The interest in words, in the power of discourse as reflected in the combination of stories, and as a vehicle of the expression of themes, is carried on into the sixth and final book with a new and more explicit focus on how the word can build a body of literature. The exaltation of the power of language and experiments with the variety of expressions that characterize the fifth book are directed and channeled in the Libro Sexto into an open discussion and apotheosis of poetry itself.

The Role of Artistic Language: Libro Sexto

Led by the figure of Telesio, himself a famous authority who is familiar with the place, all the shepherds gather at the enchanted (conventional) valley of "Los cipreses." In the middle of the valley, the presence of the Tajo River completes the idyllic scene. Like the river, the shepherds converge in the valley to participate in a cycle. They, with their songs, verses, and praises will pay tribute to the departed Meliso (68) and in so doing, to the general current of their national cultural life.

---

(67) *Ibid.* All the above examples are from the Libro Quinto. Due to the extensive treatment of the subject of language throughout the section, all specific page numbers are provided with the particular quotation. For the small "critical storm" caused by the use of the cliché "yo seguro que" see Avalle-Arce's comment and information on p. 141, n. 1.

(68) Meliso, according to the critics, is the pastoral name for the poet Diego Hurtado de Mendoza. The references of the other shepherds to the published works of this author make this supposition valid. Cf. Avalle-Arce's notes on his edition of *La Galatea, ibid.*, p. 179.

As a reward for their effort, Poetry herself, in the figure of Calliope, erects a poetic monument to the poets of their Spanish tongue. Inserted, "nested" as the many other episodes of the *Galatea*, this monument, like the river, is comprised by the streams—contributions of individual poets to the general flow. Taking from the current and adding to it, they enrich their national literature (69).

Since *La Galatea* ends with Book Six, we can take the analysis no farther, but the riches of the Canto de Caliope are more than sufficient for me to examine the role that artistic language, poetry, has in the context of *La Galatea*.

Canto de Calíope

The introductory octave of Caliope's song and some of the "octavas" dedicated to a few prominent literary authors are included here:

> *Al dulce son de mi templada lira*
> *prestad, pastores, el oído atento:*
> *oiréis cómo en mi voz y en él respira*
> *de mis hermanas el sagrado aliento.*
> *Veréis como os suspende, y os admira,*
> *y colma vuestras almas de contento,*
> *cuando os dé relación, aquí en el suelo,*
> *de los ingenios que ya son del cielo.* (Octava 1)
>
> . . . .
>
> *¿Quién pudiera loaros, mis pastores,*
> *un pastor vuestro amado y conocido,*

---

(69) I owe the association of the river image to the verbal monument inserted at the center of this Libro Sexto to Professor Alain Seznec.

pastor mejor de cuantos son mejores,
que de Fílida tiene el apellido?
La habilidad, la ciencia, los primores,
el raro ingenio y el valor subido
de Luis de Montalvo, le aseguran
gloria y honor mientras los cielos duran. (Octava 28)

. . . .

En don Luis de Góngora os ofrezco
un vivo raro ingenio sin segundo;
con sus obras me alegro y enriquezco
no sólo yo, mas todo el ancho mundo.
Y si, por lo que os quiero, algo merezco,
haced que su saber alto y profundo
en vuestras alabanzas siempre viva,
contra el ligero tiempo y muerte esquiva. (Octava 61)

. . . .

Estos quiero que den fin a mi canto,
y a nueva admiración comienzo;
y si pensáis que en esto me adelanto,
cuando os diga quién son, veréis que os venzo.
Por ellos hasta el cielo me levanto,
y sin ellos me corro y me avergüenzo:
tal es Laynez, tal es Figueroa,
dignos de eterna y de incesable loa. (Octava 111) (70)

This Canto is written in praise of famous poets, artists, and
scientists, contemporaries of Cervantes, along with some allusions to prestigious figures from Spanish literary history, including authors of the Neo-hispanic world (i.e. Francisco de
Terrazas in Octava 67). In this series of 111 laudatory *octavas*,
Cervantes stresses the merits of those responsible for the im-
provement of their country's art, while at the same time mak-

---

(70) *La Galatea*, Avalle-Arce, editor, Libro Sexto, pp. 190-225.

ing these encomiastic vignettes part of one of the recurrent conventions in pastoral aesthetics: the encomium of the poet.

From another point of view, the self-conscious attitude toward the poetic vocation serves another purpose which has not been satisfactorily discussed in the analysis of pastoral works. It stresses the reflections of the authors and pastoral characters on the poetic art itself, and explains the functions of the numerous songs praising the artistically arranged speeches of the shepherds, their singing matches, and the "conventional" insertion of "Cantos" dedicated to praising the accomplishments of poets of a given country or place, such as the present "Canto de Calíope."

What is the purpose of the complicated incorporation of earlier artistic, linguistic, rhetorical, and thematic structures? What is the meaning of the inclusion of all these expressions, themes, and authors? As we have seen in the previous analysis of the books of *La Galatea*, Cervantes succeeded in giving an integrated re-elaboration of old and new literary elements, thereby creating a new version of well-known cultural patterns within our literary tradition. He innovated by reinforcing what was part of the common domain.

The insistence on including such large numbers of fellow poets (colleagues) could be interpreted as a display of scholarship, a sense of belonging to a special intellectual group. In this sense, it is not different from the way modern scholarship is carried out in every academic field (71). Belonging to a group of poets such as those mentioned by the nymph Calliope: Gálvez de Montalvo, Góngora, and Fray Luis, the poet

---

(71) Laurence Lerner notes to this respect: "Every culture has one or more centers of social, artistic, and moral standards. . . . In the Sixteenth and Seventeenth centuries, this center was the court; by the Nineteenth it was the city; in modern America it is becoming the university. Most literature is written from and for this center." In *The Uses of Nostalgia: Studies in Pastoral Poetry*, London, Chatto and Windus, 1972, p. 20.

is, by association, held to be in direct dialogue with those figures of the literary community. In a synchronic way, this dialogue is equivalent to the association sought by quoting and imitating (diachronically) famous masters of the classical literary past. As such, it is another way of reinforcing the sense of all-inclusive *communitas* where all contribute with a personal effort.

That so many lesser-known poets and figures of the literary scene were included by Cervantes, and by the other authors in their respective pastorals, may give us pause regarding their true intentions in these encomiastic "Cantos." This would deserve a larger treatment than the space and the aim of this study permit. However, in the total context of the convention of praise as practiced by authors of pastorals of this period—not only in Cervantes but from Sanazzaro and Montemayor to Gil Polo and d'Urfé—the justification for these laudatory addresses is that the accomplishments of the successful masters enrich the individual and by association, the rest of the group and the culture as a whole. As Cervantes puts it:

En sus obras me alegro y enriquezco
no sólo yo, mas todo el ancho mundo (72)

In this sense, the poets who cultivate this art become true *authors* in the original Latin sense: the general who conquers new lands for his country (73).

Considering the complicated equivalences, reflections, and similarities, it is not inconceivable to see *La Galatea* as an example of the "roman-à-clef"; as such it has been repeatedly studied (74). While it is possible that some of the 97 shep-

(72) *La Galatea*, Avalle-Arce, editor, Libro Sexto, p. 210.

(73) José Ortega y Gasset, *La deshumanización del Arte*. Madrid, Revista de Occidente, 1960, p. 31.

(74) A good survey of this subject in Fitzmaurice-Kelly's introductory notes to the cited English edition of *La Galatea* (see especially p. xxxiv). More recently, Geoffrey Stagg in "A Matter of Masks: La

herds of the story are actual people in disguise, it is to the activity of the poet/shepherds that I address my analysis. In particular I examine here the purpose of the praise (explicit and implicit) of poets that is carried throughout the narrative.

That praises are part of a macro-contextual emphasis on a renewed cultivation of manners is well-known (75). Daniel Javitch demonstrated in a recent study (76) how Elizabethan cultivation of rhetorical forms was part of a general movement advanced by the teachings and practices of the humanistic Neo-Platonic schools of the period. This is, of course, not exclusive to that period (77) nor limited to England alone. Courtly manners and rhetorical expressions in poetry had been made important in all European countries by the enormous success of Castiglione's *Book of the Courtier* (1528). But the influence of the book was followed by a gradual change in emphasis from the proper court style to a growing faith in the exemplary powers of poetry *per se*. The Renaissance interest on rhetorical power, so thoroughly documented in recent studies such as William J. Kennedy's *Rhetorical Norms in Renaissance Literature* (1978) and Nancy Streuver's *The Language of History in the Renaissance* (1970), was an ongoing concern among intellectual

---

Galatea," *Hispanic Studies in Honour of Joseph Manson*, Dorothy M. Atkinson and Anthony H. Clark (eds.), Oxford, 1972, establishes as a fact that *La Galatea* is a roman-à-clef. Cf. Avalle-Arce, *La novela pastoril española, op. cit.*, p. 263.

(75) Cf. Renato Poggioli, *The Oaten Flute: Essays on Pastoral Poetry and the Pastoral Ideal*, Cambridge, Harvard University Press, 1975, p. 31.

(76) Daniel Javitch, *Poetry and Courtliness in Renaissance England*, Princeton, Princeton University Press, 1977.

(77) Helen Cooper, *Pastoral: Mediaeval into Renaissance*, Ipswich and Totowa, D. S. Brewer, Rowman and Littlefield, 1977, especially, pp. 4 and 5.

groups such as the members of La Plèiade (78). And that is what Cervantes was defending in the passage from the Prologue cited earlier.

This shift from the exclusive emphasis on courtly manners to a renewed claim that poets were providers of instructive models for refined conduct and entertainment, is one of the most salient, yet rarely discussed major aspects of Renaissance pastoral. Though the shift to a new vision indicates a change, this is not to say that the courtly manners were abandoned. The manners of the court were, in fact, the trademark of the communities of disguised shepherds. But it is in the art of poetry and in literary expression where the proof of the pastoral media (authors/characters/audiences) is measured.

The praise of the poet which, as we saw earlier, was directed often at individual poets (i.e. the Nicias depicted in Theocritus' Idyll IX—see Chapter III of this book) was later commonly addressed to particularly famous authors. Virgil, the "Mantuan Tityrus," is addressed in Prosa Decima of Sanazzaro's *Arcadia*, in *La Galatea*'s Libro VI, and in many others. This practice, itself considered a convention in pastoral works ever since the early laudatory laments for the archetypical poet Daphnis and for the Poet of Idyll V in Virgil, was expanded in the prose romances of the Renaissance into praise of various poets as members of a group. That is to say, they praised the institution of poetry itself, as the words of Du Bellay propose.

The praise of the poet in itself reaches at least back to Aristotelian encomiastic rhetoric and has been re-elaborated

---

(78) A. H. T. Levi quotes Du Bellay who in his *Deffense et illustration de la langue française* (1549) gives the final criterion for the poet, whose task it is to make us 'love and hate, enjoy and suffer, admire and shock," cf. "The Role of Neoplatonism in Ronsard's Poetic Imagination," in *Ronsard the Poet*, ed. by Terence Cave, London, Methuen and Co., 1973, p. 143, note 1.

ever since Virgil (79). But this convention, as in the case of others, appears with a purpose definitely more enriching than the mere imitation or the cultivation of a commonplace. As the authors themselves often repeat, their aim is to establish a new recognition of the poetic task: the creation of literary art. This is, in turn, a purposeful, concerted effort having roots encompassing even more than the tradition of Western literature. In both Oriental and Western literary traditions, the poet has been considered a prophet, the *vates* (speaker or intermediary between higher orders and humans). As the discussion of pastoral linguistic and rhetorical devices has demonstrated, authors of pastoral works show a particular awareness of the contrivances and difficulties involved in the elaboration of fiction. For fictional possibilities, not factual ones, are the key to literary art (80). In this self-acknowledged fictional art, where the poet arranges words to make his discourse communicate difficult feelings and thoughts, the poet as *vates* is seen as holding the key to the act of communication.

The addition of each poet to the general body of poetic authors places the concern with repetition of words, phrases, and names in a new light. That is, by uttering the same words, each with their individual voices, this group of poets acts in a kind of concert, where art, artists, and nature collaborate, as described in *La Galatea*:

---

(79) Aristotle in the section of his *Rhetoric* devoted to this subject, says that the true aim of laudatory rhetoric is the moral approbation and praise to men [sic] who have done something of moral value. Cf. *Aristotle's Rhetoric*, Sir Richard Jebb, editor and translator, Cambridge, Cambridge University Press, 1908, p. 42. See also fn. 10 of this chapter.

(80) Ronsard, member of La Plèiade, and author of Eclogues said in his *Franciade*: "Les poètes ne cherden que 'le possible' ou le vraisemblable, non la verité." Première Préface (1572), Hugues Vaganay edition, Paris, Garnier Frères, 1924, p. 526.

Al acabar de Tirsi, todos los instrumentos de los pastores formaron tan agradable música, que causaba grande contento a quien la oïa y más ayudándoles de entre les espesas ramas mil suertes de pintados pajarillos que, con divina armonïa parece que como a coros les iban respondiendo. (81)

But just as in the case of the characters who, saying the same words, carrying the same names, the poets are in constant competition to demonstrate the superiority of their individual discourses. They are in a keen competition to excel. They are equal but different.

It is for this reason that they emphasize euphony and discretion, the ability of authors and characters alike to show mastery and eloquence, control of the subject. In the case of some of the characters (Tirsi, Elicio), the emphasis on "discretion"—evenness of judgment and clarity of minds becomes almost obsessive. For the love-stricken shepherds of the books, control and discretion applies to the balance and control of their passions as well as to the excellence of expression (their eloquence as storytellers). Thus the praises and competition for excellence are themes that are conventional in pastorals. But these praises are there in function of the justification of the poetic art and the need for a particular kind of approach to the problems of artistic communication.

The reflection on art as giver and source of skill and eloquence is the subject of the "Canto de Calïope." The "Canto" deals with one central idea: the poetry of Spain. As with the other themes and characters of the book, the ideal of poetic art is not given a simple expression but is reflected in multiple and diverse ways. One thought articulated by different voices, one theme developed by diverse means and approaches (Fray Luis, the meditative poet; Góngora, the sophisticated *poeta culto*; Garcilaso, epitome of lyricism;

---

(81) *La Galatea*, Avalle-Arce, editor, Libro Segundo, p. 121.

Gálvez de Montalvo, model of pastoral author). We saw that Galatea—the star—is also a constellation, a group and a circle of nymphs/poetic stars. As with Galatea, they are united by a common aim and by the means of a common language. The multiple Galateas, Nísidas, Tirsis, and Damons are unified by their names, the characteristics they embody, and the feelings they all share. In the chain of poets included in the "Canto de Calíope" the one hundred names representative of the art are unified by their association with earlier masters and by the possible allusions to the characters/shepherds in the fictional text. The most important link that they all share however, is their common poetic art.

Recapitulation

Like the pastoral story of Galatea and the surrounding shepherds/poets, this study draws to a close. The *Canto* with its praises of poets epitomizes the poetic art while embodying a central convention of pastoral as well. It also epitomizes the aims of Cervantes in *La Galatea* as it ties together the stylistic and thematic conventions of the work into a larger vision of the poetic art.

Through an emphasis on artistic coherence, stylization and wit, the major authors of pastoral exploit conventions to introduce a totally fictional "reality"—a world-other-than-the ordinary. Both the authors and the audiences contribute—with knowledge and cultivation—to the realization (the fact) that they are part of a series; that they belong to a cycle or a cultural body from which they receive and to which they contribute.

The distinctions between macro-contexts and micro-contexts offered in the earlier chapters of this study and the examination of basic linguistic, rhetorical and thematic conventions of the genre all proved to be necessary in this attempt to recover the aims of pastoral in general and *La Galatea* in particular for contemporary understanding. In the end the very "conventionality" critics used to dispose of any need to understand the pastoral romances has turned out to be their essence. It is an essence, not stale and static as the term seems to suggest, but rather dynamic and alive in the works representative of the genre. In the hands of a literary artist, pastoral themes and their conventionality can be the most illuminating vehicle of the poetic art. In this way they are also testimony to the power of art to move us through fiction, often with more force than any empirical experience can.

CHAPTER VII

CONCLUSIONS

The current study is an effort at recovery. Pastoral has been at once an enormously popular set of literary forms and an unaccepted challenge for contemporary literary criticism. It is hard for twentieth century readers to imagine how audiences could have been captivated by these highly stylized, complex, and slow-moving works. Yet captivated they were. Not only did these works proliferate, but many of the acknowledged great masters of Western literature tried their hand at these forms.

The purpose of this study has been to analyze the concept of convention in pastoral and to examine the function and interrelations between some of the basic conventions of Renaissance pastoral romances. In particular, I have endeavored to show that conventional does not mean static or lacking in literary possibilities. This review has been neither exhaustive nor complete; rather I have emphasized our obligation to understand the defining characteristics of this literature variously labeled as "cosmopolitan," "highly stylized," and "conventional" and its appeal to audiences.

Since the term "conventional" does not explain the meaning and function of the different conventions employed in these romances, I distinguished among the various meanings of convention and have examined the different roles of some specific conventions in pastoral.

The principles of *vraisemblance* or coherence, the self-reflecting character of pastoral language derived from the convention of textual recuperation and the constant commentary on the role of the poet have been the major general conventions—the macro-contexts—examined in this study. The repetition of certain linguistic features (pastoral names, sentences, clichés), and certain themes (unsynchronized love, *tempus amoenus, locus amoenus*, melancholy) were selected for study as basic components—micro-contexts—of the texts. The interrelation among the different conventions, their purposes, and their consequences in the production of pastoral romances were studied through an integrated reading of Cervantes' *La Galatea*. Other examples were taken from Sanazzaro's *Arcadia*, Montemayor's *Diana*, and d'Urfé's *L'Astrée*.

The importance of distinguishing among conventions and examining their functions, of course, extends beyond the limits of the pastoral genre. The consequences of maintaining or subverting conventions, the problems we encounter in interpreting works of remote periods, and the challenges of appreciating changes in aesthetic perspectives apply to other literary forms as well.

In common with other literary genres, pastoral creates imaginary realities through the artistic manipulation of language. This artistic endeavor, in the case of pastoral, involves the set of particular linguistic, thematic, and structural conventions to construct refined models. Through these models, difficult issues, such as temporal flux and human passions, can be analyzed. This can also be accomplished by other artistic means (e.g. comedy, parody, metaphysical poetry, and many of the other genres that are part of our literary culture).

In choosing to use refined models of perfect diction, intertextuality, coherence and exalted beauty, pastoral authors do not produce exact replicas of natural reality. Rather, the violation of the principles of naturalistic art is central to pastoral, lending the genre its characteristic kind of intensity.

Pastoral romances, then, are part of a purposefully fictional literature which displays as a main characteristic a coherence between its general philosophical and aesthetic principles and the linguistic and rhetorical elements that express them. The interplay of the conventions creates a special kind of inward, self-reflecting action that moves all the elements toward a unique coherence.

The emphasis on beauty achievable by cultivation of coherence and order conforms to a worldview which seems at first to take two contradictory directions. The apparent paradox arises because the pastoral emphasis on artistic cultivation underscores a belief in the perfectibility of the world. At the same time, the very need for betterment through art (or by other means) reflects a concept of a world that, in its evolution, has become worn out, decayed. Through order and beauty, humans can achieve some control over the disorder, or at least some understanding of it. This comprehension is directed not only outward to the social and physical worlds, but also inward to the self as well. That is, the models of beauty also provide patterns of conduct.

The tension between a view of humanity moving from confusion to knowledge and one of humanity cast out in a world that is increasingly worn out and confused explains, in part, the pastoral cultivation of an aesthetic that attempts to reconcile these visions. This tension also explains the choice of the major conventional pastoral themes, particularly melancholy, which in itself related then to other themes. A sense of melancholy, nostalgia for a time now lost, compels the artist to engage in a retrospective construction of a timeless age, an Arcadian (unchangeable or categorized) *locus amoenus*, and a search for the universal Eros which will give meaning to the complex, diverse, and confusing state of human passions.

This sense of distance is accomplished not only through particular expressions and themes but also by the actual structuring of the narrative itself. The analysis of these structures is stressed in the present study. Precisely because these romances are constructed by juxtapositions of larger and smaller, finished and continuous segments, the structure can be also considered as a paradigmatic model through which things can be seen from more than one side. And because of the structuring of the narratives in accumulated stories themselves segmented by commentators, by unexpected as well as by predictable episodes, and by alternating voices, these pastoral romances provide a particular multifaceted way of dealing with difficult issues.

Both internal audiences (listening characters) and external audiences (readers) are always placed at the vantage point of an observer—a point from which they can watch everyone and listen to everyone's reported experiences. From being an observer, the audience (particularly the internal one) passes to being judge, advisor, and ultimately, participant. This also happens in the case of the reader, albeit in different measure.

Another characteristic of pastoral narrative structure also emphasizes aesthetic distance. Though ordinary empirical time is generally perceived as a continuous line, the fictionalization of real experiences and real events is presented in pastoral as constant interruptions in the narrative. Through these discontinuous segments—or *lapsi* which Lindenberger calls "idyllic moments" (1)—particular problems can be contrasted and analyzed. The same result is also achieved by moving events in space to "natural" retreats.

The retreat to those privileged moments and spaces is achieved, in these romances, by a structural segmentation that, at times, is accomplished by shifts from prose to verse,

---

(1) Herbert Lindenberger, "The Idyllic Moment: On Pastoral and Romanticism," *College English* 34 (1972):335-351.

or just as frequently by the interjection of new characters or of the commentators' remarks. In all cases, these temporal and spatial displacements are expressed through a continuous display of orderly, euphonic means of expression and of erudition through the inclusion in the discourse of the voices and expressions of the Classical authors of pastoral.

In my analysis of *La Galatea*, I have brought out the different conventions, examining their interactions and functions in this particular pastoral romance, treating it as a representative work for the analysis of the poetics of pastoral. A "nested" reflection of reflections, interpolations, excerpts, corresponding names, roles, stories, and parallel vignettes is achieved in this Cervantine work. With multivaried voices, the shepherds/poets of *La Galatea* tell selected excerpts of their sentimental lives. In these "personal" stories, each of the characters is witness, protagonist, subject, and object of the action. The effect of these stories, echoing the *roto espejo* metaphor, is of harmonious disharmony or disharmonious harmony that entertains and holds our interest while composing the central thread of the book.

In *La Galatea*, we thus have a work that is embedded in a tradition: one of creating beautiful models of eloquence and balance. Cervantes demonstrates his knowledge of the literary aims of the pastoral tradition and his skills at literary recuperation by interweaving past models of classical and vernacular literature (Virgil, Tasso, Garcilaso, Castilian traditional songs). The result is a literary work which adds to the flow of literary culture, appropriating from it by adapting elements and returning to it a new interpretation of earlier questions. In this sense, the image of the river/monument contained in the "Canto de Calíope" (described by one critic as a "boring catalog") (2) has the function that the author (through his or

---

(2) Marcel Batillon, "Relaciones literarias," in Juan Bautista Avalle-Arce and E. C. Riley, editors, *Suma Cervantina*, London, Thamesis Books (1973), pp. 215-232.

the "Muse's" words) announced: to enrich, not only the poet, but the whole *communitas*.

This complicated contextual, intertextual, and historical reflection on contemporary poets is an accomplishment of Cervantes and a display of the power that the skillful use of the pastoral conventions may attain. His aim, as he himself repeatedly expressed, was to make obvious, to update and to upgrade the merits and efforts of his national literary art.

Cervantine critics, as we saw in Chapter VI, rightly point to the clear relationships between this pastoral work of Cervantes and pastoral works of other authors. My intention here has been to provide a renewed sense of the use and purposes of these re-elaborations of earlier works. Rather than considering this peculiar quotation and reproduction from earlier works as mere exercises in imitation or as part of a passing fad, I have examined these re-elaborations and their implications through a general "macro-contextual" approach to art, and through the individual way Cervantes applied these conventions in his work. This analysis of creation by incorporation and interweaving of new works into the collective current of the linguistic and artistic tradition has been central to my analysis of *La Galatea*. It is also my claim that it is central to any attempt to understand pastoral literature.